JN090740

Tokyo:
A Walking Tour

Akiko Matsuoka

John Turrent

装　　幀＝寄藤文平　垣内 晴

＊本書掲載のイラストマップは、実際の地図とは縮尺が異なります。ご紹介している施設周辺
　地域の様子を知る参考としてご覧ください。また掲載されている店舗、博物館等の情報は
　2021年1月時点のものです。内容が変更になる場合もありますので、おでかけの際には事前
　に確認することをおすすめいたします。

＊本書の制作にあたり、取材、撮影等にご協力いただきました皆様にお礼申し上げます。

＊写真協力：中野正貴（秋葉原）　斎藤太郎（浅草・上野）　足成（東京スカイツリー）
　　　　　　塚田満雄（原宿・明治神宮・秋葉原）

＊翻訳協力：マイケル・ブレーズ　エド・ジェイコブ

＊編集協力：iTEP Japan

通訳ガイドがナビする

東京歩き

【新版】

Tokyo：A Walking Tour

Akiko Matsuoka

松岡明子＝著

John Turrent

ジョン・タラント＝訳

目　次

CONTENTS

まえがき

　私は東京のど真ん中育ちです。東京タワーが完成した頃、150メートルの展望台まで階段を駆け上ったり、皇居に隣接している日比谷公園になぜかあった吊り輪で鉄棒のぶら下がり練習をしたりしました。銀座のデパートも遊び場でした。現在、海外からのお客様をガイドしている原点は、そんな子供時代に経験した東京でのわくわくした気持ちを伝えたいからかもしれません。私の家の近くにはオランダ大使館があり、その頃から外国への興味を持ち始めていました。そして通訳ガイドになることが夢になったのです。

Preface

I grew up right in the middle of Tokyo. Around the time when Tokyo Tower was completed, we would run up the stairs as far as the observation deck, 150 meters high. In Hibiya Park, adjacent to the Imperial Palace, there were, for some reason or other, some gymnastic rings, and we would use them to practice swinging from the bar. The department stores in Ginza were our playground, too. Probably the starting point of my present career as a guide for foreign visitors to Japan was my desire to convey to them the thrills that I experienced myself during my childhood in Tokyo. The Embassy of the Netherlands was situated near our home, and my interest in foreign countries was kindled early on. My dream was to become a guide interpreter.

難関の通訳ガイド国家試験に受かってから現在に至るまで、失敗は数知れずあり、思い出すと今でも心臓がドキドキしてきます。上野の東京国立博物館に特別休館日（月曜が祭日の場合の翌日火曜日）に行ってしまったり、ある水曜日、朝5時起きしてお連れした築地魚市場が閉まっていたり！ さらには初めての大役で、パーティーの司会をしたときのことです。あまりの緊張で、乾杯の音頭を、あろうことか、なんと自分でしてしまいました！ 当時、私がガイドしたお客様にはなんとお詫びをしたらよいのか、世界中を行脚したいくらいです。

　アジア某国の王女様のご一行を空港でお出迎えするとき、先頭を歩いてこられる随行の方を発見し、丁寧に英語でご挨拶、ご案内を始めたところ、その方は某大手日本企業の現地日本人社長でした。日焼けしたそのお姿からすっかり現地の方と間違えてしまったのです。周りからの冷たい視線に冷や汗が出ました。

　とんちんかんなあわてものガイドでしたが、持ち前のノリのよさと気の弱さからくるやさしさがお客様に気に入ってもらえるようになり、2年目にして、ツアー終了後、ギリシャのお客様から往復航空券が届きま

After passing the difficult state examination for guide interpreters, especially in the early years, I made countless blunders that even now make my heart skip a beat. Once I took a group to the Tokyo National Museum only to find it closed. (The museum is closed on Mondays except if that day is a national holiday, in which case it closes on the following Tuesday!) One Wednesday I got up at 5 a.m. and took everyone to the Tsukiji fish market, but it was closed! And then there was my first important job as an emcee at a party. I was so nervous that when it came to proposing a toast, I went and did it myself of all things! I still feel as though I should make a redemptive pilgrimage around the world to apologize to the guests at that time.

And once, when I went to the airport to meet the entourage of a queen from a certain Asian country, I politely greeted the person walking at the head of the group in English and began to give an explanation, only to find that he was the Japanese president of a major Japanese corporation's affiliate in that country. He was so tanned, I had mistakenly thought that he was a local member of the entourage. The cold looks from those around me certainly sent shivers down my spine.

I was an inarticulate, bumbling, novice guide, but guests seemed to like my enthusiasm and kindness born of a timid character. In my second year, after the end of a tour, a Greek customer sent me a dreamlike present—a roundtrip airline ticket to Greece. That

した。夢のようなギリシャ旅行のプレゼントでした。これでその後のガイド人生が決まってしまいました。

　毎年日本を訪れる外国人は増えています。外国人と話をしていて、話題が日本の歴史や文化になったとき、答えに詰まってしまうことはないでしょうか。仏教と神道の違いは？　天皇と将軍の関係は？　明治維新って何？　おすすめの観光地は？　日本ならではのお土産は？　など、当然日本人なのだから知っているはずと聞かれたとき、すぐに答えられなくて恥ずかしく思ったことはありませんか。

　通訳ガイド（通訳案内士）は二者間の話を通訳するのではなく、自分自身で話の内容を組み立ててガイドをすることが主な仕事です。日本各地の観光地や国立公園などの景勝地を外国人とともに旅をしながら、自然のなりたちの説明をしたり、各地の伝統文化や現代の生活ぶりなどをご紹介したりと、多岐にわたる話題を分かりやすく、興味を引くようにガイドしなければなりません。

　通訳ガイドになりたての頃はガイドのテキスト文を丸暗記し、マイクを握り締めて必死にしゃべりまくっていました。お客様からは、単刀直入に素朴な質問がぽんぽん

was when I finally decided that being a guide was the career for me.

The number of foreigners visiting Japan is increasing year by year. I am sure you have experienced talking with foreigners and finding it difficult to answer when asked about Japanese history or culture. What is the difference between Buddhism and Shinto? What was the relationship between the emperor and the shogun? What was the Meiji Restoration? What tourist spots do you recommend? What souvenirs do you recommend? And so on. No doubt, like me, you have felt ashamed at your inability to reply, even though the foreigner expects you to know because you are, after all, Japanese.

A guide interpreter does not only interpret the conversation between two other parties. The main task is to prepare your own talk and serve as a guide. While traveling with foreigners to Japanese tourist spots, national parks, and other scenic places, you must explain the workings of nature and introduce local traditional culture and modern lifestyle. You must be prepared to talk about a wide range of topics in an easy-to-understand and interesting manner.

When I was just starting out as a guide interpreter, I used to memorize guide texts by heart and grip the microphone tightly as I rattled away. The people on the bus would then ask simple questions, and as

飛び出し、あわてているうちに説明したかった建物も通り過ぎ、何の話題だったのかも解らなくなる始末です。しかし、だんだんとコツをつかんで、質問される前に先回りをしてガイドするようになると、やっとマイペースで楽しくガイドできるようになりました。日本を客観的に見る習慣もつきました。遠く海を越えてわざわざ訪日されたお客様の心を受け止め、日本に感動していただくためにはどうしたらよいのか？

　まずは日本を自分なりに多面的に見直してみる。そして、子供がよくする「なぜ？」という質問を自問自答しつつ、やがて日本を再発見することが大切だと気づきました。感性を磨き、出会った方々の文化的背景や、個人的な興味を探り出して、無理のない糸口を見つけて、話題を選び相互の感性の交流ができることを心がけるようになりました。

　そんな私が、マイクを持つ手をペンに換えて、本書にて、30数年のキャリアを通して得た日本の首都、「東京」の見方、歩き方、多少のうんちくを語りつつ、皆様を東京ツアーへとご案内いたします。一人でも多くの方が、海外の方々とご一緒に、楽しみながら、東京の魅力を再発見し、伝統を再認識し、多様な文化を満喫していただけたらと願っております。

　本書の作成に、ゼロからすべてのご指導とご支援をいただいた(社)国際交流サービ

I groped for answers, the building that I wanted to explain about would disappear from view behind us, and I would lose the thread completely. Gradually, however, I came to learn the ropes, to anticipate questions before they came, and eventually to work enjoyably at my own pace. I also developed the habit of looking objectively at Japan. I asked myself how I could understand the minds of foreigners who come such a long way and make them impressed by Japan.

First of all, I took another look at the many sides of Japan myself and asked myself, as children frequently do, why? And I realized that it was important to rediscover Japan. I came to try hard to polish my senses, understand the cultural backgrounds and personal interests of the people I met, find discreet threads, and choose topics carefully so that we could exchange feelings.

Now, putting down my microphone for a while, I have written this guide to Tokyo, the capital of Japan, using the information about sightseeing and walking around and the tidbits of knowledge that I have picked up from more than three decades of working as a guide. I hope that it will be of help to readers, foreigners and Japanese alike, in rediscovering Tokyo, reconfirming its traditions, and enjoying its diverse culture.

I would like to take this opportunity to express my sincere gratitude to Takashi Ushiyama, the editor

ス協会の季刊誌Café編集長牛山貴氏、日本語のあいまいな部分までもみごとに本意を汲んで英訳をしてくださったジョン・タラント氏、出版に際し、原稿の提出の遅れにも辛抱強くおつき合いくださり、温かいアドバイスとご指導をいただいたIBCパブリッシング社の編集長浦晋亮氏、編集担当の賀川京子氏に心より感謝申し上げます。

　最後に、本書を執筆するにあたって、多くの示唆に富む情報をご提供くださった、NPO法人通訳ガイド＆コミュニケーション・スキル研究会（GICSS）の研修講師の皆様、さまざまな助言をしてくれた家族に感謝の意を表したく思います。

2014年4月
松岡　明子

　本書第1刷から早や10年以上が経ち、新たに発見される東京の魅力も増え、この街を歩く目的も多種多様です。たとえば、古き美しきデザインを保存・復元しつつ、耐震構造も確保された新・東京駅舎と、その目の前、皇居へといざなう行幸通り周辺は筆者一押しの新風景となりました。

　さて、東京歩きの第一歩に本著が皆様のお供としてご一緒できることを願っています。いってらっしゃい！

in chief of *IHCSA Café*, the quarterly newsletter of the International Hospitality and Conference Service Association, who gave me sound guidance and assistance right from the start of this project; to John Turrent, who translated the Japanese text most proficiently, even adding necessary explanations in English where the Japanese might be somewhat ambiguous for foreigners; and to editor in chief Kuniaki Ura and editor Kyoko Kagawa of IBC Publishing, who waited patiently even when I was late submitting the manuscript and offered me kind advice and guidance.

Finally, I would also like to express my appreciation to the training instructors of the Guide Interpreting & Communication Skill Studies Association (GICSS), who supplied me with much stimulating information, and to my family, who gave valuable advice.

April 2014
Akiko Matsuoka

More than 10 years have passed since the first printing of this book, and as more and more of Tokyo's charms are discovered, there are more reasons for walking around the city. For example, the new Tokyo station building, which preserves and restores the beautiful old design and has an earthquake-resistant structure, and the area around Gyoko-dori, which leads to the Imperial Palace, have become my favorite new sights. I hope that this book will accompany you on your first steps in Tokyo. Enjoy your walk!

粋な浅草から東京スカイツリー (1)

Starting with Edo Culture:
From Asakusa to Tokyo Skytree

↑ for Tsukuba
筑波方面

Asakusa View Hotel
浅草ビューホテル

Kokusai-dori
国際通り

Kappabashi
合羽橋

Asakusa Station
浅草駅

Kappabashi Kitchenware Street
かっぱ橋道具街

Shinbori-dori
新堀通り

Tsukuba Express (Subway)
つくばエクスプレス

↓ for Akihabara
秋葉原方面

← for Ginza
銀座方面

Tawaramachi Station
田原町駅

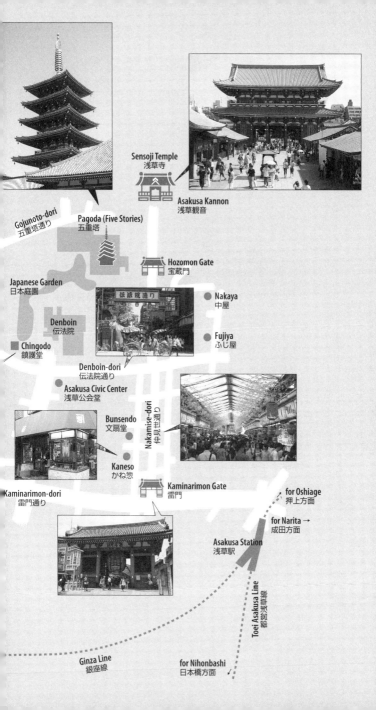

Sensoji Temple
浅草寺

Asakusa Kannon
浅草観音

Gojunoto-dori
五重塔通り

Pagoda (Five Stories)
五重塔

Hozomon Gate
宝蔵門

Japanese Garden
日本庭園

● **Nakaya**
中屋

Denboin
伝法院

● **Fujiya**
ふじ屋

■ **Chingodo**
鎮護堂

Denboin-dori
伝法院通り

● **Asakusa Civic Center**
浅草公会堂

Bunsendo
文扇堂

Nakamise-dori
仲見世通り

● **Kaneso**
かね惣

Kaminarimon Gate
雷門

for Oshiage
押上方面

Kaminarimon-dori
雷門通り

for Narita →
成田方面

Asakusa Station
浅草駅

Toei Asakusa Line
都営浅草線

Ginza Line
銀座線

for Nihonbashi
日本橋方面

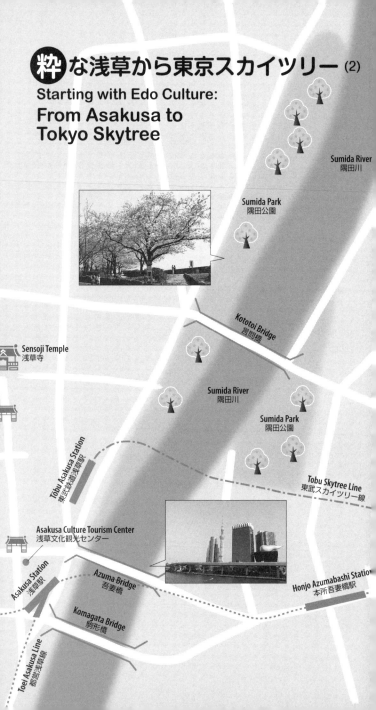

粋な浅草から東京スカイツリー (2)

Starting with Edo Culture:
From Asakusa to Tokyo Skytree

Sumida River
隅田川

Sumida Park
隅田公園

Kototoi Bridge
言問橋

Sensoji Temple
浅草寺

Sumida River
隅田川

Sumida Park
隅田公園

Tobu Asakusa Station
東武鉄道浅草駅

Tobu Skytree Line
東武スカイツリー線

Asakusa Culture Tourism Center
浅草文化観光センター

Asakusa Station
浅草駅

Azuma Bridge
吾妻橋

Honjo Azumabashi Station
本所吾妻橋駅

Komagata Bridge
駒形橋

Toei Asakusa Line
都営浅草線

for Kitasenju ↑
北千住方面

Hikifune Station
曳舟駅

Keisei Hikifune Station
京成曳舟駅

for Aoto, Shibamata
青砥、柴又方面

TEMBO GALLERIA (450m)
天望回廊

TEMBO DECK (350m)
天望デッキ

Tokyo Skytree
東京スカイツリー

Tobu Isezaki Line
東武伊勢崎線

Keisei Oshiage Line
京成押上線

Tokyo Solamachi
東京ソラマチ

30F, 31F
Skytree View
スカイツリービュー

5F
Sumida Aquarium
すみだ水族館

4F
Ginza Natsuno
銀座夏野

Oshiage Station
押上駅

Tokyo Skytree Station
とうきょうスカイツリー駅

Toei Asakusa Line
都営浅草線

Hanzomon Line
半蔵門線

N

浅草

　1590年に江戸へ入城し、その後1603年に将軍となった徳川家康が取り組んだ事のひとつは、戦国時代が終わって、雑兵としての仕事を失った日本中の若者たちをいかにして新規開発事業に巻き込むかでした。イタリアのベニスにヒントを得た家康が目指したのは、さまざまな職業の人間が造る活気のある商業都市でした。そして、城や堀を造る土木建築職人、江戸湾の魚介類を捕り加工する漁師、日常生活に必要な道具を作る職人などによる江戸の町造りが本格的に動き出し、江戸の町は、その後さらに大都会東京へと発展していったのです。

　東京の原点はまさに江戸にあります。東京を楽しむためには**江戸情緒**が欠かせません。そして江戸文化を色濃く残し、東京で一番人気がある観光名所といえば、なんといっても浅草です。

浅草寺

　浅草・浅草寺の観音様をお参りする人は年間3000万人、そのうち950万人が外国人。昔から参詣人のお目当ては、観音様のご利益もさることながら、楽しい仲見世通りでの買い物だったのです。それも、表通りのお土産店だけでなく、一本裏手の通りに入ったり、ちょっと横丁

仲見世通り

Asakusa

Tokugawa Ieyasu (1543–1616) entered Edo Castle in 1590 and received the title of shogun in 1603. The Edo Period (1603–1868) ushered in a peaceful society in which many young men lost their former posts as low-ranking soldiers. Ieyasu thus launched a project to involve as many of them as possible in new urban development projects. Inspired by Venice in Italy, Ieyasu aimed to create a vibrant commercial city built by people of diverse vocational backgrounds. Thanks to the efforts of artisans who built Edo Castle and its moats, fishing folk who caught marine life in Edo Bay and processed it into seafood, artisans who created essential goods for daily living, and other specialists, the town of Edo underwent full-fledged urban development and gradually evolved into the Tokyo metropolis.

Since the origins of Tokyo lie in the city of Edo, a **familiarity with Edo** is crucial to appreciating Tokyo. In that sense, Asakusa retains strong remnants of Edo culture and is Tokyo's most popular sightseeing spot.

Every year 30 million people, 9.5 million of whom are non-Japanese, visit Senso-ji Temple in Asakusa, where a statue of Kannon, the goddess of mercy, is enshrined. Since Edo times, as well as to worship before the statue, visitors have come here to enjoy shopping along the Nakamise-dori, the approach to the temple. In the shops that line this street, and

浅草文化観光センター
台東区雷門2-18-9
03-3842-5566
年中無休
（メンテナンス等による休館を除く）

の角を曲がってみると、そこに本当の浅草の魅力、代々受け継がれた職人の手作りの品々、**匠の技**に出会います。

　雷門をすぐにめざしたいのですが、はやる心を抑えてまずは浅草の全容が見渡せるスポットをおすすめします。真向かいにある浅草文化観光センターです。新国立競技場や現代の東京の姿を変えてきた建築家、隈研吾がデザインを手がけ2012年にリニューアルしました。**浅草界隈**には伝統的な平屋家屋がまだまだ健在ですが、その平屋を積み木のごとく縦に積み上げたデザイン、外壁は不燃加工を施した杉の集成材でできている8階建の黒い建物です。

　1階で浅草全体地図をゲットした後はぜひ8階展望テラス（無料）に上ってみてください。仲見世通りが一列に緑の屋根を見せながらつながり、その先に浅草寺の宝蔵門、その左に**五重塔**そして**本堂**が見渡せます。五重塔はその耐震性がいまだに明らかではないのですが、大地震でも決して倒壊しないという事実が物語る先人の知恵の結晶です。視線を右方向に移すと東京スカイツリーが見えます。隅田川をはさんで伝統の五重塔と最新技

also in the adjacent side roads and alleyways, you will find the real attractions of Asakusa—the handmade products and **craftsmanship of artisans** carrying on long traditions.

Although you may feel the urge to head straight for Kaminarimon, I recommend controlling that impulse and first visiting a vantage point from which you can get a panoramic view of Asakusa. That spot is the Asakusa Culture Tourism Center, just across the way. The building is the work of Kengo Kuma, the architect who designed the New National Stadium and changed the face of modern Tokyo. It was renovated in 2012. In the **environs of Asakusa** there are still a good many traditional one-story Japanese homes, and the Center looks for all the world as if a number of these homes have been built one on the top of the other, like building blocks. The outer walls consist of noninflammable laminated cedar, and there are a total of eight stories, all done in black.

After getting a map of the Asakusa vicinity on the 1st floor, be sure to go up to the 8th floor observation terrace (free of charge). From there you can see the line of green-roofed shops along Nakamise-dori leading to the Hozomon Gate of Sensoji, and to the left are the **five-story pagoda** and the **main hall**. The secret behind the pagoda's imperviousness to earthquakes is still a mystery, but the fact that it has withstood the severest quakes is testament to the expertise of its ancient architects. If you direct your line of sight to the right, Tokyo Skytree comes into view. On one side

術の東京スカイツリーが対峙しているここからの風景はまさに温故知新。一見に値します。

まずは雷門から仲見世通りを本堂に向かって歩きます。合計90あまりの店舗があり、長さは約250メートル。享保年間（1716 ～ 1735）の頃、浅草寺を訪れる**参拝客**が増えるにつれて、境内の清掃を課せられていた近隣の人々に対して、境内や参道上に出店営業の特権が与えられたのが仲見世通りの始まりとか。

雷門：浅草寺の総門。江戸初期の建立後、3回の火災に遭い、現在の門は1960年再建。

ぜひ立ち寄りたいのは雷門からひとつ目の交差店を左へ曲がった角、140年の歴史を誇る和包丁を商う刃物店かね惣です。お目当ての包丁が決まるとその場で研いでくれます。研ぎの名人芸を見て楽しむもよし、あるいはぶらぶらして20 ～ 30分後に戻れば研ぎあがった世界一よく切れる包丁を手にすることができます。使ってみると、お料理の腕は確実に一段上がります。

かね惣
台東区浅草1-18-12
03-3844-1379
不定休

文扇堂
台東区浅草1-30-1
03-3844-9711
20日過ぎの月曜日
（月1回）定休

投扇興：箱枕状の台に蝶のような的をおき、1.6メートルほど離れて座ったところから扇を投げて的を落とす。落ちた形や位置で点数をつける江戸時代の優雅な遊び。

また、その反対側には舞扇専門店。江戸時代に始まった優雅なお座敷遊び、投扇興（とうせんきょう）のセットも扱っています。ところで浅草は江戸時代の頃から**花街**と共存共栄の間柄でした。本堂の前にかかっている

of the Sumida River you have a traditional pagoda, on the other side the Tokyo Skytree, fruit of the latest technology. This is a bona fide example of man's learning from history and is well-worth seeing.

First of all, walk from Kaminarimon Gate along Nakamise-dori toward Kannon Hall, which is the main hall of Sensoji Temple. Some 90 shops line this 250-meter street. Around the Kyoho Era (1716–1735), due to the increased numbers of **worshippers** visiting Sensoji Temple, local residents who were ordered to clean the grounds of the temple received the special privilege of opening shops within the temple grounds or along its approach. These shops eventually turned into the Nakamise-dori shopping street.

After passing under Kaminarimon Gate and turning left on the first side street, there on the corner is one shop you must visit: Kaneso, a cutlery store that has been selling Japanese kitchen knives for 140 years. Once you decide which knife you want, you can have it sharpened on the spot. You can enjoy observing a veteran artisan's sharpening expertise while you wait, or you can visit nearby shops for 20–30 minutes and then return to pick up your just sharpened knife, featuring the world's keenest cutting edge. Using this knife will definitely enhance your culinary skills!

Across the street, there is a store selling fans for use in traditional Japanese dance. This store even sells sets of fans for playing the fan-throwing game, an elegant parlor recreation that began during the Edo Period. Incidentally, from Edo times Asakusa coexisted and

大きな提灯は、今でも新橋の芸者さんたちが数年おきに奉納しているものです。

　一方、扇子（せんす）は芸者さんたちの踊りには欠かせない道具。さてその扇子ですが、もともとは朝鮮から伝わった高貴な女性が顔を隠すための団扇（うちわ）のようなものでした。日本でも高松塚古墳壁画に描かれた飛鳥美人が手にしています。木製で重かったものを、細い木片の骨に紙を張って軽くし、持ち運びやすく折りたたみができるように改良しました。そして扇子が誕生しました。平安時代初期9世紀ぐらいのことです。

　この軽く、コンパクトにするプロセスはまさに**日本のお家芸**のようです。その後、16世紀の大航海時代にポルトガルやスペインの航海者たちが扇子をヨーロッパに紹介したのです。上流階級の夫人たちが愛した東洋の扇子はその後庶民にも行き渡り、ついにアバニコと呼ばれるフラメンコダンサーが手にする扇になりました。

　彼女たちの華麗で優雅な踊りに欠かせないツールであるアバニコのルーツが日本だったとは驚きですね。グローバライゼーションのはしりでしょうか。

　さて、仲見世通りに戻り、本堂に向かって進むと左手に伝法院通りの看板が見え

coprospered with **entertainment districts**. Even now, the large lanterns in front of the main hall are donated every few years by the geisha of Shinbashi.

An indispensable item for geisha dancing is the **fan**. Originally, it seems, the fan came to Japan from Korea, where it was used by noble women to conceal their faces. In Japan also, one of the women drawn in the wall paintings of Takamatsuzuka Tomb in Asuka, Nara Prefecture, dated to around AD 700, appears to be holding a fan. Wooden fans were heavy, so over time, improvements were made in Japan to create lighter fans that were easier to carry (by covering ribbed frames with paper). The *sensu*, or folding fan, another Japanese invention, appeared around the ninth century, during the early Heian Period (794–1185).

Making things lighter and more compact is obviously a **forte of the Japanese**. After that, in the sixteenth century, during the Age of Great Voyages, voyagers from Portugal and Spain introduced folding fans to Europe. First of all upper-class ladies found them exotic; then they became popular among common people as well, and eventually they became the model for the *abanico* fan used by flamenco dancers.

Yes, the abanico, an essential implement in that beautiful and elegant dance, actually has its roots in Japan. In a sense, therefore, the folding fan was a forerunner of globalization.

Now, return to Nakamise-dori and walk a short distance toward Kannon Hall until the sign for

伝法院通り

てきます。18世紀には百万都市になった江戸では商業も発達し、**名物**やさまざまな生活用品などを売る専門店もたくさん現れました。商品や店名を宣伝するために店の前に暖簾を下げたり、屋根の上に看板を掲げ、ひと目で商売が分かる工夫をこらしたのです。

伝法院通り沿いのお店の袖看板は江戸時代にならってそれぞれの屋号や商品をかたどったデザインが施されています。デザインを楽しみながら進んでください。すると、びっくり! 思わず足を止めてしまいます。呉服屋さんの屋根の上に、今にも動き出しそうなねずみ小僧の人形です。

東側も江戸時代の景観に改修されており、道の真ん中で目をひくのは可動式の台車に乗った歌舞伎18番の白浪五人男の一人日本駄右衛門、あとの4人は屋根の上やバルコニーで睨みをきかしたり見えをきっています。まるで歌舞伎の舞台を見ているようです。

有名人の手形

江戸切子やアンティーク着物のお店も並びます。通りの中ほどにある浅草公会堂前の歩道に、ハリウッドをまねた日本の有名人の手形がはめ込んである通りがあるのはご愛嬌。その先に、**明治維新の**

Denboin-dori comes into view. In the eighteenth century, as Edo grew into a city with a population of one million people and commerce flourished, many stores appeared selling **specialties**, everyday goods, and so on. In order to advertise a product or the store's name, the store would hang a *noren* (small entrance curtain) outside or place a sign on its roof so that people would know instantly their line of business.

The shops on Denboin-dori have signboards designed in the shape of their names or products à la Edo style. Look out for them as you walk by. There is one especially that is sure to stop you in your tracks. On the roof of a kimono store, a doll representing the famous thief Jirokichi the Rat (Nezumi Kozo) seems about to come alive.

The east side, like the west, has been renovated in the Edo style, and one's attention is immediately caught by the sight of a mannequin of the Kabuki character Nippon Daemon on a cart—Daemon being one of a band of honorable thieves dubbed the Five Men of White Waves. The other four are perched on rooftops and balconies, striking poses and glaring down at the people below. It is almost as if you are watching an actual Kabuki performance.

Also nearby are shops selling Edo cut glass and antique kimonos. Halfway down the street, in imitation of Hollywood, the handprints of Japan's celebrities are preserved in the sidewalk in front of the Asakusa Civic Center. Just beyond stands Chingodo, a

おたぬき様

折に、伝法院を火災から守る約束をした**守り神**「おたぬき様」を祭る鎮護堂があります。実はそのちょっと横手から浅草寺本坊である伝法院のお庭が見渡せます。このお庭は小堀遠州作といわれています。

助六
台東区浅草2-3-1
03-3844-0577
無休

また仲見世通りに戻ってみましょう。宝蔵門の手前、右側の江戸玩具の店助六もはずせません。江戸時代末期の**ぜいたく禁止令**のもと、玩具もできるかぎり小さく手作りした時代の伝統の技を伝える江戸小玩具の店です。すべてが手作りです。この店の**犬張子**は上皇后美智子陛下が皇后雅子様へ安産を祈ってプレゼントしたことで知られています。

中屋（本店）
台東区浅草2-2-12
03-3841-7877
無休

本堂に向かう前に、宝蔵門の手前を右へ曲がった角にお祭り道具専門店中屋があります。お祭り好きな浅草っ子がお祭りの日に身につけるものすべてがそろうお店です。本物の半被を目にすることができます。

ふじ屋
台東区浅草2-2-15
03-3841-2283
木曜定休

さて、そのまま本堂とは逆方向に歩いて数軒目に、染手拭い専門店ふじ屋があります。木綿の手拭いはさまざまな使いみちがありましたが、今では風景、動物、

Shinto shrine dedicated to the *tanuki* (raccoon dog), the **guardian deity** who pledged to protect Denboin Temple from fire during the turbulent years of the **Meiji Restoration**. Denboin is the main temple of the Sensoji Temple complex. From slightly to the side, you can look out over the garden of the temple, said to have been designed by the multitalented artist Kobori Enshu (1579–1647).

Let's return again to Nakamise-dori. Don't miss the Edo toy shop Sukeroku, located on the right side of the street in front of Hozomon Gate. Selling toy miniatures, this shop inherits traditional artisanship from an era when—in conformance with **sumptuary laws** legislated in the final years of the Edo Period— even toys had to be made as small as possible. All the miniatures are handmade. This shop's **paper-mâché dogs** are famous because Her Majesty the Empress Emerita Michiko presented one to Her Majesty the Empress Masako during her pregnancy to wish her an easy childbirth.

Before heading back to Kannon Hall, turn right just before Hozomon Gate and visit the Nakaya shop on the corner. Nakaya offers every type of festival apparel worn during festivals by the local Asakusa residents, who are well known as avid festival aficionados. Here you can see genuine traditional festival *happi* coats.

Walking past several shops in the direction opposite Kannon Hall, you will come upon Fujiya, a shop specializing in dyed *tenugui* (towels). Although cotton tenugui were traditionally put to various

花々、歌舞伎などなどデザインのおもしろさと美しさでまさに芸術品ともいえます。額に入れて楽しむのもおもしろいでしょう。

かっぱ橋道具街

　伝法院通りをそのまま進み、国際通りに出ます。浅草ビューホテルを右に見ながら真っすぐ進むこと15分ほどで食品サンプルで外国人に人気のかっぱ橋道具街に到着です。和洋食器、厨房器具、暖簾専門店など170店余りが800メートルにわたって並んでいます。

　日本のレストラン入り口のショーウインドーに並べられる食品サンプルは、メニューが読めない、と困り果てる外国人には大変重宝されています。日本人ならではのきめ細かい合理的なディスプレイを見れば、外国人も安心して入店できるというわけです。そして、そのサンプルを本物よりもおいしそうに精巧に作る日本の知恵と技に、外国人は感心しきりなのです。

　食品サンプルは以前はロウ、現在は主にプラスチックで作られます。帰国後、

practical uses, they are presently enjoyed as works of art due to their interesting designs and beauty, featuring landscapes, animals, flowers, Kabuki actors, and other motifs. One way of appreciating tenugui is to hang a framed tenugui on the wall.

Kappabashi Kitchenware Street

Keep going along Denboin-dori and you reach Kokusai-dori. With the Asakusa View Hotel on the right, walk straight ahead for about 15 minutes and you come to Kappabashi Kitchenware Street, which is popular among foreigners for its plastic food samples. The 800-meter road is lined by about 170 stores selling such things as Western and Japanese cutlery, kitchenware, and noren curtains.

The plastic food samples that Japanese restaurants display in show windows at their entrances are very useful for foreigners who cannot read the Japanese menus and are often hesitant to step inside. Upon seeing the customer-friendly displays, they can go in and order without anxiety. What is more, the samples themselves are made so well, they can look even more delicious than the real thing. Foreigners are often awed by this product of the wisdom and skill of the Japanese.

In the past these food samples were made of wax, but now they are mainly plastic. They make fun

食品サンプル

自宅でのパーティーで自慢の料理が並ぶテーブルにお遊びで日本土産の食品サンプルを置き、気がついたお客の驚く顔が見たい！ 大好物の握り鮨が文字盤に並び、**割り箸**でできた針が回って時を告げる鮨時計をキッチンの壁にかけたい！ こんな遊び心を持つ外国人に大人気の買い物ストリートです。日本滞在中にレストランや料亭で見かけた珍しい物、たとえば、鳥型のレモン搾り器、玩具のようなわさび用のおろし金、一人用の七輪なども見つかるのです。お料理好きにとってはキッチングッズにあふれた夢のようなお買い物天国です。

人力車に乗って浅草界隈を
回るのも一興。

souvenirs, too. How about taking one back with you and placing it on the table when you host a dinner party at home? Imagine the looks of astonishment on the guests' faces when they realize what it is! Or you could hang a sushi clock on your kitchen wall using plastic samples of sushi and **disposable wooden chopsticks** as hands! Kappabashi shopping street is very popular among foreigners with such playful minds. You will also be able to find those fascinating rarities that you noticed at Japanese-style restaurants during your stay in Japan, such as lemon squeezers shaped like a bird, a toy-like wasabi grater, and a *shichirin* for one. For people who like cooking, Kappabashi is a shopper's paradise.

東京スカイツリー

　2012年5月、東京の空の風景が一変しました。東京スカイツリーの完成です。自立式電波塔としては世界一の高さ634メートル、3万2000トンの鉄骨づくりです。約2万5000の部材が工場や現場で溶接され4年弱の工期を経て東京の新しい**観光名所**になりました。紅白の色に塗られている兄貴分の東京タワーと違い、薄い銀色に輝く鉄塔はこの大都会の青空に調和して美しくその存在を誇っています。

　高層ビルが立ち並ぶ東京からデジタル放送電波を発信するためには、東京タワーのほぼ2倍の高さが必要となりました。耐震構造は伝統の心柱理論を採用、超高速のエレベーターは350メートルの**天望デッキ**まで50秒（秒速600メートル）です。

東京スカイツリー
墨田区押上1-1-2
03-5302-3470
年中無休

Tokyo Skytree

In May 2012 the Tokyo skyline underwent a dramatic transformation with the completion of Tokyo Skytree. At 634 meters and 32,000 tons, the steel-constructed Skytree is the tallest free-standing tower in the world. Approximately 25,000 parts were welded together in factories or on-site, and the construction process was completed in a little less than four years, making Skytree Tokyo's newest **sightseeing attraction**. In contrast to the older Tokyo Tower, which is painted in red and white, Skytree is a faint steel gray that harmonizes beautifully with the city's blue skies.

In order to enable digital broadcasting from Tokyo with its many high-rise buildings, it was necessary to have a structure nearly twice the height of Tokyo Tower. The earthquake-resistant construction relies on a traditional central shaft, and the express elevators reach the lower 350-meter-high Tembo Deck (**observation deck**) in 50 seconds (at 600 m/s).

ドアが開くと突然の天空世界。1320万人が住む大都会東京の姿を鳥になったつもりで楽しんでください。そして、展示してある「江戸一目図屏風」は**必見**です。隅田川の先に江戸城、方角も視点もほぼまったくこの天望デッキから見下ろしている風景です。江戸時代の絵師はどうやってこの風景を描くことができたのか?! と思いは広がるばかりです。

　2013年に世界文化遺産になった富士山は20近くの都県から見ることができるとのことです。単純計算で富士山が見える都県の人口を合計すると約4000万人にのぼります。日本人の3人に1人が富士山の見える地域に住んでいる計算です。北は福島県阿武隈山脈の日山、西は和歌山県色川富士見峠、南は八丈島といわれています。

　さて、東京スカイツリーは、少なくとも都内なら少し高い建物で見る方角が正しければどこからでも見えます。おすすめは浅草寺の境内から見える姿です。そして、浅草観光のあと、東武線でひと駅「とうきょうスカイツリー駅」から直結であっという間に足元に到着です。また、東京メトロ半蔵門線「押上駅（スカイツリー前）」からのルートは、ツリーの足元からエスカレーターを乗りついでソラマチの4階に到達します。だんだんと近づ

When the door opens, you suddenly find yourself in the heavens, so to speak. You can enjoy a vista of Tokyo and its 13,200,000 people as if you were a bird. A **must-see** is the screen-painting of Edo on display showing a panorama of the town with Edo Castle seen beyond the Sumida River, nearly the same angle and view as from the observation deck. It makes one wonder how the painters of the Edo period could have achieved this bird's-eye view.

It is said that Mt. Fuji—designated a World Cultural Heritage Site in 2013—is visible not only from Tokyo but from some 20 prefectures around the country. This adds up to some 40,000,000 people, meaning that one out of three Japanese lives in an area with a view of Mt. Fuji. In the north, it can be seen from Mt. Hiyama in the Abukuma Mountain Range in Fukushima prefecture, in the west from Irokawa Fujimi-toge in Wakayama prefecture, and in the south from the island of Hachijojima.

As for the Tokyo Skytree, it can be seen in Tokyo from any fairly tall building, as long as you are looking in the right direction. The recommended view is from within the grounds of Sensoji Temple. After enjoying sightseeing in Asakusa area, you can take the Tobu line one stop to Skytree Station and from there you soon find yourself at the foot of the Skytree. Or, another way is to take the Tokyo Metro Hanzomon line to Oshiage Station (Skytree Mae), from which you take an escalator to the 4th floor of the Solamachi commercial complex. This route creates a sense of

いてゆく楽しさがあるルートです。

東京スカイツリー
webチケット
https://www.tokyo-
skytree.jp/ticket/
individual/

入場は当日券以外に、外国人優先券購入も可能です。一般価格より1100円ほど高額ですが、休日など混雑時にはおすすめです。パスポート提示が必要。通訳ガイドも同額で同行できます。

銀座夏野
東京ソラマチ4階
03-5610-3184

イーストヤード4階に和風土産物店が数軒あります。銀座に本店がある**箸専門店「銀座夏野」**。東京スカイツリーをかたどった木製箸は数色、夜空を飾るライティングの紫と青がおすすめです。江戸の伝統の美の紫と粋なブルーに思いをはせながら新たに登録された**世界無形文化遺産**の和食に舌鼓をうってみるのはいかがでしょうか。

天気の良い日は、より空に近づける450メートルの天望回廊に上ってみてください。別途入場料金が必要ですが、チケットは天望デッキで購入してください。通路の幅は2.4メートル。かなり狭いです。エレベーターを降りたあと、スロープ状になっている展望台を巡りながら110メートルを歩ききると高度5メートルを登り最高地点に到達する趣向です。足元まで**透明のガラス**で覆われているのでまるで空中を歩いているような浮遊感覚が味わえます。

天望デッキ

excitement as you grow nearer and nearer to your final destination.

In addition to same-day tickets, it is also possible to purchase priority tickets for foreigners. The price is about 1,100 yen more than the general price, but it is recommended for holidays and other crowded times. A passport is required. An interpreter guide can accompany you for the same price.

There are a good number of Japanese-style souvenir shops on the 4th floor of the East Yard. One is Ginza Natsuno, which **specializes in chopsticks** and is headquartered in Ginza. You can choose between several colors of Skytree-shaped chopsticks, but I recommend purple and blue, the colors in which the tower is illuminated at night. As you enjoy the traditional purple or the chic blue, you can treat yourself to traditional Japanese food, just recently designated an **Intangible World Cultural Heritage**.

When the weather is good, you should definitely go up to Tembo Galleria (the skywalk) on the 450-meter observation deck to get an even more spectacular view. An additional entrance fee is required, which you can buy at the observation deck. Getting out of the elevator, you find that the skywalk, a fairly narrow 2.4 meters, is constructed on a slope, so that as you stroll along its 110-meter length, you gain another five meters in height to reach the highest point on the observation platform. Even the windows wide open to the floor level is made of **transparent glass**, giving you the feeling you are floating in the air.

開業直後にVIPのお客様と訪れた際は、雲に覆われてなにも見えず高所恐怖症を隠しおおせてほっとしたのでした。ところが、ほどなく床に**かすかな揺れ**が。係の方に恐る恐る聞いたところ、時々少し揺れているが、問題はないとのこと。日本の技術力を信じましょう！

　お帰りの前にもう一度カメラに収めたいと思ったら東京ソラマチの1階からソラマチひろばにでて車道を横切って「おしなり橋」のたもとからローアングルでどうぞ！

When I accompanied some visiting VIPs to the tower shortly after its opening, the view was hidden by clouds, and thanks to that, I was able to keep my fear of heights a secret. However, it wasn't long before I noticed the floor was **swaying slightly**. With my heart in my mouth, I asked an attendant about it, and he said that the floor did sway a little now and then, but it was nothing to worry about. I decided to put my faith in Japanese technology.

If you want to take one final photo before leaving, from Solamachi's first floor you can go out to Solamachi Square, cross the street, and take a low-angle shot from the foot of Oshinari Bridge.

川を渡って江戸めぐり：両国、深川

Deeper into Edo:
Ryogoku and Fukagawa

Kokugikan
国技館

← **for Akihabara & Shinjuku**
秋葉原・新宿方面

Ryogoku Stati
両国駅

Hanzomon Line
半蔵門線

Sumida River
隅田川

Kiyosumi Park
清澄公園

✓ **for Nagatacho & Shibuya**
永田町・渋谷方面

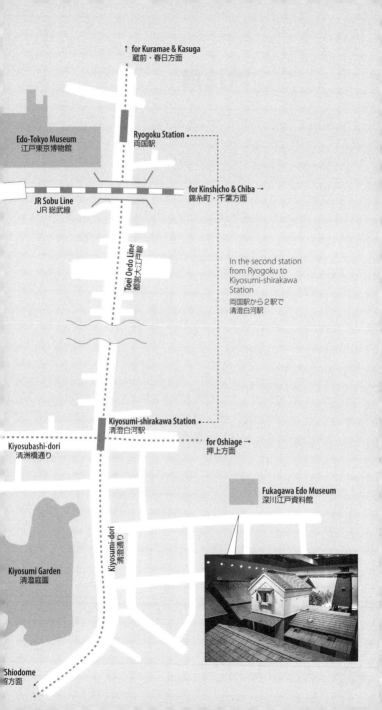

↑ **for Kuramae & Kasuga**
蔵前・春日方面

Ryogoku Station •----
両国駅

Edo-Tokyo Museum
江戸東京博物館

for Kinshicho & Chiba →
錦糸町・千葉方面

JR Sobu Line
JR 総武線

Toei Oedo Line
都営大江戸線

In the second station
from Ryogoku to
Kiyosumi-shirakawa
Station
両国駅から2駅で
清澄白河駅

Kiyosumi-shirakawa Station •----
清澄白河駅

Kiyosubashi-dori
清洲橋通り

for Oshiage →
押上方面

Fukagawa Edo Museum
深川江戸資料館

Kiyosumi-dori
清澄通り

Kiyosumi Garden
清澄庭園

Shiodome
汐方面

国技館

国技館
墨田区横網1-3-28
03-3623-5111

最初の国技館は、明
治42 (1909) 年両国
に開設された。その
後一度は蔵前に移転
したが、85年に現在
の横網に再移転され
た。

江戸NOREN
墨田区横網1-3-20
www.jrtk.jp/
edonoren/
03-6658-8033
1月1日・2日、施設
点検日 定休

　浅草から始まった小さな旅、もっと
どっぷりと江戸に浸っていただきます。
格差社会の広がりが懸念されている現代
の日本ですが、**身分制度**があったにもか
かわらず、人々が生き生きと元気よく、
そして賢く生きていた時代、それが江戸
時代です。江戸情緒を求めて両国へと隅
田川を渡ってみましょう。

　JR両国駅をおりると相撲の本場、国技
館は目の前です。駅舎を出て左へ進みブ
ルーの大きな暖簾のあるその名も「江戸
NOREN」に立ち寄ってみましょう。観
光案内所の奥には、蕎麦、天ぷら、寿司、
など、きどらない和食レストランが並び
ます。吹き抜けのホールの中央に目をむ
けると、10トンの土でできた本物と同サ
イズの土俵が目に入ります。ここでも**神
聖な場**として立ち入りは不可ですが、写
真スポットとして喜ばれます。

　両国国技館では、初場所の1月、夏場
所の5月、秋場所の9月の年3回、本場所
が開催されています。場所の様子は全国
に生中継されますが、相撲のダイナミッ
クさは、何と言っても実際の土俵の前で
見るにかぎります。

　歴史をたどると相撲に関わるさまざま
な疑問がすっきりします。

Ryogoku Kokugikan

Our trip around Tokyo started in Asakusa. Now let's go even deeper into Edo. In present-day Japan there is much concern about the widening income gaps in society, but back in the Edo Period, despite a very clear-cut **class system**, people lived energetically, cheerfully, and wisely. Our journey takes us across the Sumida River to Ryogoku in search of this Edo esprit.

After exiting JR Ryogoku Station, the Kokugikan, the home of sumo, will be right in front of you. As you exit the station building, turn left and stop by a food hall whose name, Edo Noren, comes from the large blue entrance curtains called *noren*. Behind the Tourist Information Center, you will find a variety of casual Japanese restaurants, including soba, tempura, sushi, and more. In the center of the atrium, you will see a ring made of 10 tons of clay, the same size as a real ring. This is also a **sacred place** and visitors are not allowed to enter, but it makes a great photo spot.

The Ryogoku Kokugikan stages three *basho*, or tournaments, a year: in January, May, and September. Although these days the bouts are televised live nationwide, you can only really appreciate the full dynamism of sumo by watching it up close.

The answers to many of the questions that you will have concerning sumo can be found in its history.

まわし（廻し・回し）：
土俵入りの際に締める
儀式用として、「化粧ま
わし」もある。外国では
Sumo belt と呼ばれる
ことも。

まずは力士の正装について。なぜ、力士たちはまわしだけの姿なのでしょうか？ それは武器を隠し持たず、文字通り裸一貫で勝負をする気概が込められた姿なのです。鍛え上げた身体に、**清浄のしるし**としてまわしのみをつけているのです。昔は、天皇や神様へ奉納する相撲の競技者である力士自身が清められた神聖な存在だったということです。

日本最古の歴史書である古事記や日本書紀には、神々がどのようにこの国を創造したのか、天皇家のルーツなどが語られています。その中に天皇の前で神々が、力比べの死闘を繰り広げたという相撲の起源を思わせる記述があります。後にはその年の**農作物の収穫を占う**神社での祭りの儀式として、相撲が執り行われるようになりました。

現在の相撲の魅力である伝統的作法は、長い歴史を経て完成されたものなのです。力士は土俵へ上がる前に口をすすいで身を清め、土俵の上では悪霊を祓うために**塩を撒き**、病や災害をもたらす邪気を地面に踏みつけるために**四股を踏**み、土俵に蹲踞して神様への挨拶である柏手を打ちます。スポーツとして楽しむだけでなく、儀式のように繰り広げられる伝統的様式美に注目してください。**礼節**と真剣勝負が混在する日本の国技に

For example, why is it that the wrestlers wear only loincloths, or *mawashi*? Well, the wrestlers grapple with each other as near naked as possible in order to show that they are not hiding any weapons. They wear only mawashi as a **sign of the pureness** of their well-trained bodies. In the past, the wrestlers, the performers of sumo, dedicated themselves to the emperor and to the gods, and were revered as purified and sacred beings.

Japan's oldest historical documents, the *Kojiki* (Record of Ancient Matters) and the *Nihon Shoki* (Chronicle of Japan), both compiled in the eighth century, tell how the gods created this country, the roots of the imperial family, and so on. There is one description of the gods testing their strength against each other in front of the emperor. This has been taken to be the origin of sumo. Later on, sumo was held as a ritual at shrines to **pray for a bountiful harvest** that year.

The ritual that is the attraction of sumo today was shaped through a long history. Before entering the ring, the sumo wrestler rinses his mouth to cleanse his body. In the ring, he **throws salt** to ward off evil spirits, **stamps his feet** so as to push the bad air that causes diseases and disaster into the ground, and, **squatting**, claps his hands as a greeting to the gods. Sumo can be enjoyed not only as a sport but also as an aesthetic tradition. It is rather apt that Japan's national sport should be such a strange wonderland, combining **punctilious etiquette** and intense combat.

相応しい不思議なワンダーランドです。
ふさわ

　相撲部屋の朝稽古の見学もおすすめで
す。毎朝、朝食前の各部屋の土俵では、
はげしい稽古が行われています。特にぶ
つかり稽古では、身体から湯気を出した
下位の力士が、先輩力士に力いっぱいぶ
つかっていきますが、押し出す前にヘト
ヘトになってしまいます。

　親方は土俵脇の一段高い座敷に座って
厳しい指導を繰り広げます。その同じ座
敷に見学者も通されます。張り詰めた雰
囲気と迫力に息もつけないほどですが、
相撲の厳しさに触れることができる体験
です。両国には50余りの相撲部屋があり
ます。事前に電話予約をしてお出かけく
ださい。

江戸東京博物館

　さて国技館を通り過ぎて、その隣に巨
大な建物が勇姿を見せます。江戸東京博
物館です。古墳時代の穀物倉をイメージ
した外観、60メートルのその高さはかっ
て江戸城にあった**天守閣**と同じです。風
が心地よく吹き抜ける3階の入館券売り場
から展示フロアへと向かうエスカレーター
に吸い込まれてゆくのは米を狙うねずみ
ならぬ知的好奇心にあふれた皆さんです。
　館内は実物資料と大小の模型により、

江戸東京博物館
墨田区横網1-4-1
03-3626-9974
毎週月曜、年末年始
定休
(祝日が月曜の場合は
開館、翌日休館)

You are also recommended to watch morning practice at a **sumo stable**. Every morning before breakfast, the sumo wrestlers take part in rigorous practice in the stable's ring. In *butsukari-geiko*, a junior wrestler, steam pouring from his body, charges into a senior wrestler and pushes him back and forth until the junior wrestler is exhausted.

The stable master, or *oyakata*, sits on a raised floor to one side of the ring giving stern instructions. Visitors are allowed into this area, too. The tense atmosphere and gusto are sure to take your breath away, but it is a wonderful opportunity to experience the full vigor of sumo. There are about 50 stables in the Ryogoku area; make a reservation by phone beforehand.

Edo-Tokyo Museum

The large building adjacent to the Kokugikan, cutting a rather gallant figure, is the Edo-Tokyo Museum. Modeled after a rice granary in the burial-mound era, the exterior has a height of 60 meters, the same as the **donjon** of Edo Castle in the past. An escalator takes the inquisitive visitors up from the ticket office on the airy third floor to the exhibit floors.

Inside, visitors can follow the transition of the city

江戸から東京へと移りゆく生活の変化がビジュアルで楽しめます。見るべきものは山とあり、たっぷりと2〜3時間はかけたいのですが、これだけは見てもらいたいスポットを2、3ご紹介します。

　1590年から始まった江戸の町造りですが、城や大名屋敷の建設に始まり、商人や職人が住む八百八町も成長の一途をたどり、18世紀には100万人の人口を抱える大都市に変貌したのです。人々が元気に行き交う様子を再現する日本橋や両国橋の模型が展示フロアの6階と5階にあります。それぞれ800体の模型に、1500体余りの人形が江戸の人々の**喜怒哀楽**をそのままに生き生きとその中に設置されています。これらの人形を見ると、今や世界一のアニメーション大国であり、フィギュア大国でもある日本の技術を目の当たりにするようです。費用は1体5〜10万円もかかったとか。用意された双眼鏡でじっくりご覧ください。

　城や堀、大名屋敷、商店などを造る土木建築職人、行灯など日常生活に必要な道具を作る**指物師**、当時の重要な情報媒体である木版画製作工程、江戸の華といわれた火事の際に大活躍した火消し組などさまざまな人々の生活がよみがえってくる展示の中に、情報交換に利用されたユニークなものを見つけました。街角に

from Edo to Tokyo through exhibited artifacts and models both large and small. There are many things to see, so plan on spending two or three hours here at least. Introduced here are two or three exhibits that must not be missed.

The building of Edo began in 1590. The first structures to go up were the castle and the daimyo (feudal lord) mansions, after which came the many communities where merchants and artisans lived. By the eighteenth century Edo had transformed into a large city with a population of one million people. On the sixth and fifth floors of the museum (you start at the upper floor and go down), there are models of the Nihonbashi and Ryogokubashi bridges that reproduce the vitality of that time. These models feature 800 and 1,500 miniature figures, respectively, that express the **range of emotions** of Edo citizens in a lively manner. In these figurines one can also sense the high level of Japanese animation and figurine production today. Each figurine cost from ¥50,000 to ¥100,000 to make. Use the binoculars that are available to get a close look at them.

The many exhibits bring to life the various people who lived in Edo — the carpenters who built the castle, moat, daimyo residences, stores, and so on; the **cabinet makers** who made the paper-covered lamp stands and other furniture necessary for daily life; the woodblock-print artists, who provided an important information medium at the time; and the fire brigades that went into action to fight Edo's

置かれた**迷子標**です。江戸社会の一面が感じられます。迷子が発見されると親が見つかるまで発見した町の人々が扶養義務を負ったので、一刻も早く親を探さねばならなかったのです。そこで街角に石柱を建て、一面には捜している迷子の名前を紙に書いて貼り、別の面には発見された子供の情報が貼られました。巧みな情報交換の仕組みです。

丁稚奉公：商家などに住み込みで働き、礼儀作法から商人としてのノウハウを叩き込まれる。給与ではなく、衣食住が支給される。

　子供といえば当時は**丁稚奉公**。その奉公の様子が、三井越後屋の模型内に表現されているのでお見逃しなく。模型の正面からその左側に回ると、番頭さんが呉服屋で働く小僧さんに、売り場での挨拶の仕方を教えている様子が見て取れます。

　江戸東京博物館では、日本語はもちろん、英、西、仏、独、伊、中、朝語によるボランティアガイドの方々が活躍中です。ガイドについては事前に問い合わせをしてご確認ください。

frequent fires. Among these exhibits, there is one that shows a unique means of exchanging information — a **stone marker for lost children** that was placed on a street corner. This exhibit gives a valuable glimpse into one aspect of Edo life. When an Edo citizen found a lost child, he or she was obliged to act as that child's guardian until the parents could be found, so it was necessary to search for the parents as quickly as possible. Thus, stone pillars were constructed on street corners. Parents who were looking for lost children wrote their names on paper and pasted them on one side of the pillar; people who had found lost children pasted information on the other side. It was a clever way of exchanging information.

Speaking of children, as an example of the **apprentice system** of that time, don't miss the scene in the model Mitsui-Echigoya Kimono Store. In the back room on the left, a head clerk is instructing an apprentice lad about how to greet customers at the sales counter.

There are tours led by volunteers at the museum in not only Japanese but also English, Spanish, French, German, Italian, Chinese, and Korean. Please inquire beforehand about the availability of these guides.

清澄庭園

さて江戸東京博物館を出て、清澄通り沿いの大江戸線両国駅から2駅で清澄白河駅に到着します。そこは当時、墨田川をはさんで江戸の漁師、材木商の住居や、多くの物資を貯蔵した蔵が林立していた深川の中心地です。駅から歩いて3分、江戸にその人ありといわれた大商人、紀伊国屋文左衛門の別邸があったとされる地に、三菱財閥の創始者岩崎弥太郎が造った名園、清澄庭園があります。日本各地からの奇岩珍石を配して造られた下町のオアシス、水鳥の安息地でのひとときのお休みを楽しんで、深川江戸資料館へ向かいましょう。

紀伊国屋文左衛門：
江戸中期、幕府御用達商人として巨万の富を築いた (1669-1734)。

清澄庭園
江東区清澄2・3丁目
03-3641-5892
(清澄庭園サービスセンター)

Kiyosumi Garden

After leaving the Edo-Tokyo Museum, go to Ryogoku Station on the Oedo Line, which is on Kiyosumi-dori, and take the subway to Kiyosumi-shirakawa Station, two stops down the line. This is the central area of Fukagawa, a district that, in the Edo Period, straddled the Sumida River and was crowded with houses of fish dealers, timber merchants, and warehouses storing all kinds of materials. Three minutes' walk from the station there is Kiyosumi Garden, built by Yataro Iwasaki, the founder of the Mitsubishi zaibatsu, on a site where the merchant Kinokuniya Bunzaemon, a well-known figure in Edo, is said to have had a second home. Kiyosumi Garden has unusual rocks brought from all over Japan and is an oasis in the *shitamachi* district. It is also a resting place for water birds. After stopping for a breather in Kiyosumi Garden, let's head on to the Fukagawa Edo Museum.

深川江戸資料館

庭園から清澄通りを挟んで反対側に茶色の**櫓**（やぐら）が2基建っているのが、深川江戸資料館の目印です。櫓の間を進んでゆくとちょっとタイムスリップしたかのような懐かしい町並みが広がります。100メートルほど歩くと目指す深川江戸資料館、その向かい側には深川の有名人、**ちょんまげ**を結った高橋さんの「江戸みやげ屋たかはし」があります。誰にでも気さくに話しかける下町人情あふれるご主人、そしておばさんは町の人気者。外国人とも言葉は通じなくても**江戸大道芸・からくり芸**で心を通わせることができる方です。このお店では漁師町だった深川ならではのあさりの佃煮が名物ですが、昔の日本玩具もお土産にどうぞ。

深川江戸資料館
江東区白河1-3-28
03-3630-8625
第2・4月曜日休
（祝日と重なる場合は
翌日）

江戸みやげ屋 たかはし
江東区三好1-8-6
03-3641-6305

さて、1840年頃の深川、佐賀町の一角を実際の建材を使って実物大に忠実に再現した町が体育館のような大きな建物にすっぽり収まっているのがこの資料館の特徴です。一歩展示フロアに踏み込んだらまずは右側の屋根の上をご覧ください。白黒ぶちの猫がひと声上げて歓迎のご挨拶をしてくれます。お見逃しなく。フロア全体の音響、照明の変化で1日を

屋根の上の猫

Fukagawa Edo Museum

The landmarks for the Fukagawa Edo Museum are two brown **turrets** standing on opposite sides of Kiyosumi-dori. Walk between these turrets, and you come to a nostalgic townscape that is like a journey back in time. About 100 meters along the road stands the museum that we are looking for. On the other side of the road there is the Edo Omiyage-ya, a souvenir store operated by a man with a **topknot** hairstyle named Takahashi-san. He speaks affably with everyone and anyone and exudes the shitamachi spirit, and he and his wife are popular in the community. Although Takahashi-san might not be able to chat with foreigners, he can amuse them and communicate through **Edo street performances** and tricks. The specialty of Takahashi-san's store is simmered clams — naturally, since Fukagawa was once a fishing district — but you might like to buy a traditional Japanese toy as a souvenir as well.

The Fukagawa Edo Museum is a large building resembling a gymnasium in which the space is filled by a faithful reproduction, using the actual construction materials, of a part of the Saga-cho district of Fukagawa as it was in 1840. Stepping onto the exhibition floor, first of all look up at the roof on the right, where you will see a black-and-white spotted cat greeting visitors with a voiced welcome. Not to be missed! Another feature of this museum is

深川の漁師の住まい

15分間で体感できる趣向もこの資料館ならでは。

　当時江戸に暮らす人の7割は**長屋**住まいでした。一人の生活に必要なスペースは畳1帖あれば十分と、狭い部屋で肩寄せあっての暮らしですが、高床式の座敷は雨の日でも快適。張り出した屋根から露地の真ん中に掘った溝に雨水を落とし、下水として流す。このみごとな処理法は、当時のパリやロンドンよりも清潔で疫病などに悩まされなかった**江戸の知恵**そのものです。

　清潔な日本の象徴といえば、高速道路の休憩所のトイレにも設置してあるハイテクトイレットです。その開発秘話を紹介すれば、長いバスでの移動で話題に困った時も大うけです。開発会社の社員が一丸となり、愛社精神のもと、さまざまな課題をクリアして、究極の製品ができあがったのは1980年。その後、今やほぼすべての日本の新築家屋に設置されるようになり、はたまた、床が濡れていない、新幹線や高速道路のサービスエリアのトイレは、自慢のメイド・イン・ジャパンです。

that changes in the acoustics and lighting on the floor as a whole enable visitors to experience a full day in just 15 minutes.

The people of Edo, 70 percent of whom lived in **row houses**, thought that a space of one tatami mat was quite sufficient for a person to live, and they resided shoulder-to-shoulder in narrow rooms. Nevertheless, the raised-floor houses were ideal on rainy days. Rainwater was dropped from the overhanging roofs into a drain dug in the middle of the alley in order to wash away the sewage. This wonderful example of recycling reflects the **wisdom of Edo**, which was cleaner than cities like Paris and London at the time and not troubled by outbreaks of the plague or other diseases.

Speaking of hygiene, the high-tech toilets that are installed in rest stops on expressways are symbolic of Japan's cleanliness. The little-known story behind the development of these toilets is a great conversation topic for a long bus ride. It was in 1980 that the employees of the company that developed them created the finished product after overcoming various challenges through unity and loyalty to their firm. Since then, the products have been installed in almost all new homes built in Japan, and the toilets that keep floors clean in Shinkansen bullet trains and highway service areas are proudly made in Japan.

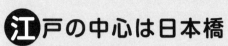

江戸の中心は日本橋

The Heart of Edo:
Nihonbashi

↑ for Ueno & Asakusa
上野・浅草方面

Edo-dori
江戸通り

Muromachi 3-chome
室町三丁目

Ginza Line
銀座線

Mitsukoshimae Station
三越前駅

Bank of Japan H.Q.
日本銀行

Mitsui Main Building
三井本館

Sotoboru-dori
外堀通り

Mitsukoshi Dept. Store
三越

← for Nagatacho & Shibuya
永田町・渋谷方面

Hanzomon Line
半蔵門線

Mitsukoshimae Stat
三越前駅

Nihonbashi F
日本橋川

for Nakano
中野方面

Tozai Line
東西線

N

Ozu Washi
小津和紙

Ibasen
伊場仙

for Oshiage →
押上方面

Nihonbashi Bridge
日本橋

Edobashi Bridge
江戸橋

Metropolitan Expressway
首都高速道路

Nihonbashi Station
日本橋駅

↓ **for Ginza**
銀座方面

日本橋

　江戸は地方から仕事を求めてきた人々や徳川家に仕える武士たちが生き生きと闊歩（かっぽ）する町でした。世界一の商業都市、武家政治の本拠地を造ることを夢見た徳川家康は、魚河岸（うおがし）、米や紙、薬などの生活必需品の市場が開かれていた川端に架かる小さな橋に、江戸橋ではなく、なんと「日本橋」という大胆な名前をつけてしまいました。そして、そこを基点としてというよりはその橋が終着点となる、つまりはすべての道はローマではなく江戸へと人々を引き寄せるために、日本各地へと延びる5つの街道を整備しました。はたして、400年前のもくろみは成功し、現在、日本橋は**その名に違わぬ**日本の中心地として堂々と生き残りました。

五街道：東海道、中山道、甲州街道、奥州街道、日光街道の5つの街道をさす。

　現在の日本橋は1911年に架け替えられたものです。ルネッサンス様式の石造り二重アーチ橋です。日本橋から西へ、東海道の終点京都三条大橋までは503キロ、大阪までは550キロ、鹿児島までは1469キロと橋のたもとの道標にあります。それでは橋のどこからこの距離は測られるのでしょう。実は橋の真ん中に埋め込まれている50センチ四方の日本国道路元標からです。年に1回、車輌の通行

Nihonbashi

Edo developed into a bustling city, full of people who had come looking for work from the provinces and samurai loyal to the Tokugawa family. Tokugawa Ieyasu, the first shogun in the Edo Period, dreamed of building Edo into the world's foremost commercial city and the center of samurai government, and he grandly named the small bridge linking riverside markets selling fish, rice, paper, medicine, and other daily necessities, not "Edobashi," or bridge of Edo, but Nihonbashi — bridge of Japan. Moreover, Ieyasu had five highways connecting Edo with other important parts of the country constructed with this bridge as, not the starting point, but the finishing point. In other words, he was proclaiming that "all roads lead not to Rome but to Edo." Ieyasu's plan four centuries ago was a success, and Nihonbashi Bridge survives to this day as, **true to its name**, the center of Japan.

The present Nihonbashi Bridge, a Renaissance-style, stone, double-arch bridge, was built in 1911 to replace the old one. A signpost at the foot of the bridge indicates that to the west, it is 503 kilometers to Sanjo-Ohashi Bridge in Kyoto, the terminus of the Tokaido highway; 550 kilometers to Osaka; and 1,469 kilometers to Kagoshima. You might wonder exactly where on the bridge these distances are measured from. Well, in the middle of the bridge there is a 50-centimeter-square post marking the "zero milestone"

をいったん遮断し、近隣の方々がきれい
に掃除をするそうです。

　日本橋は**文化財**にも指定されている橋
ですが、現在は首都高速道路が覆いかぶ
さるように上を走っています。1964年
の東京オリンピック開催のために日本橋
川沿いに造られた高速道路は、今も大都
市東京の大動脈として大きな役割を果た
している一方で、**文化の香り高い建造物**
である日本橋を容赦なく覆いつくしてし
まっているのです。

　しかし、この橋の上に青空を取り戻す
ために総工費3200億円をかけ、高架線
を1.2キロに渡って地下に移設する計画
が始動しました。新宿の都庁建設費用の
ほぼ2倍とは驚きですが、完成予定は10
年か20年先とのこと。東京の新たな景観
が現実味を帯びてきました。

日本橋

　中央通りを北へ、創業（1673年）以
来多くの**日本初**のサービスを発信してき
た百貨店、三越へ向かいましょう。三越
の前身である越後屋は、「**現金掛け値な
し**」というスローガンで初めて店頭で着
物の定価販売を行う事により信用と人気
を得、呉服なら越後屋というブランドを
手にしました。その後明治時代にはフラ
ンス製の自動車による配達サービスを開
始。1904年に三越呉服店となり、翌年の

三越
中央区日本橋室町
1-4-1
03-3241-3311
定休日なし

spot. Once a year local people apparently halt traffic across the bridge in order to clean this milestone.

Nihonbashi Bridge is designated as a **cultural property**, but today it is dwarfed by an elevated expressway running overhead. This expressway, which was built at the time of the Tokyo Olympics in 1964 and runs parallel to the Nihonbashi River, certainly plays an important role today as a transportation artery for the Tokyo metropolis, but it mercilessly cast a shadow over Nihonbashi Bridge, a structure **with a strong cultural fragrance**.

However, a plan has been launched to relocate the elevated highway underground for 1.2 kilometers at a total cost of 320 billion yen in order to restore the blue sky over this bridge. The cost of this project may seem surprising since it is almost double the cost of the construction of the Tokyo Metropolitan Government Building in Shinjuku, but it is scheduled to be completed over 10 or 20 years. Tokyo's new cityscape is becoming a reality.

Let us head north along Chuo-dori to Mitsukoshi Department Store, one of the leading department stores in Japan and the setter of a number of **first-in-Japan** records since its founding in 1673. Echigoya, the predecessor of Mitsukoshi, gained trust and popularity as the first store in the country to sell kimonos at fixed prices under the slogan of "cash and **no extra charges**," and its brand image — "If you want a kimono, go to Echigoya" — became firmly established. In the Meiji Period (1868–1912) Echigoya

ライオン像

デパートメントストア宣言以来、エスカレーター日本初導入、劇場開設、地下鉄乗り入れなど新しい試みを続け、今でも日本橋地域開発の中心です。堂々としたルネサンス式の建物やライオン像は、日本橋のシンボルになっています。

　三越のすぐ裏手、江戸時代に**金座**があった地にひときわ威容を誇る日本銀行があります。明治政府が新都市東京の姿を作ってゆく時、多くの近代的建物の設計を託したのはイギリス人建築家のジョサイア・コンドルでした。しかし、明治をむかえ、**日本通貨価値の安定**を図るため紙幣を印刷、発行する国立の日本銀行を設計、建設したのは、コンドルの弟子であった辰野金吾でした。堅固な石と煉瓦で1896年に完成しました。江戸が東京に生まれ変わるときの、いわば、締めくくりを託されたのです。明治人の気概に思いを重ねてみてはいかがでしょう。

日本銀行
中央区日本橋本石町
2-1-1
03-3279-1111

重要文化財に指定されている本館の見学ツアーも実施されている。
予約は03-3277-2815まで。

日本の中央銀行。日本の金融、経済の中枢を担う。

began a delivery service by means of a French-made automobile. In 1904 it became Mitsukoshi Kimono Store, and the following year it declared itself to be a department store. After that, among many other things, Mitsukoshi became the first department store in Japan to install escalators, open a theater, and provide direct subway access. Even today, Mitsukoshi is still at the center of community development in Nihonbashi, and the majestic Renaissance-style building and lion statues at its entrance have become a symbol of the district.

Just behind Mitsukoshi, the Bank of Japan stands proudly on the site where the **gold mint** was located in the Edo Period. When the Meiji government was building the new city of Tokyo, the British architect Josiah Conder was entrusted with the design of many of the modern buildings. However, it was Conder's apprentice, Kingo Tatsuno, who designed and built the Bank of Japan, the national bank that printed and issued banknotes to **stabilize the value of Japanese currency** at the start of the Meiji Period. It was completed in 1896 using solid stone and brick. You might say that the bank was entrusted with completing the rebirth of Edo as Tokyo. Think about how much spirit the people of the Meiji Period had.

幕末の頃、日本の**金銀比価**は金1に対して銀5（1：5）と国際比価（1：13）とは大きな違いがありました。たとえば、海外から日本に持ち込まれた5グラムの銀を1グラムの金と交換し、その1グラムの金を上海や香港で銀に交換すると13グラムの銀になる。その13グラムの銀をまた日本で金と交換すると3グラム弱の金になる。あっという間に3倍近くの利益が生まれるわけです。加えて、海外から持ち込まれた洋銀と国内の高価値の銀とが同種同量の原則に基づき両替されることから起こる貨幣両替の混乱、大量の金貨流出、**物価の高騰**などの問題が経済の混乱を生み、ひいては明治維新の引き金になったともいわれます。

　それでは次に、終焉が近い頃の徳川幕府の懐具合を推測させるものが残っているスポットを訪ねてみましょう。中央通りに戻り、歩みを進めて三越から北に進み、2つ目の交差点を右へ曲がると大伝馬本町通りに入ります。この通りこそ実は、当時江戸で一番の繁華街、メインストリートであり、多くの大店が立ち並ぶ美しくも活気あふれる町並みが広がっていたのです。残念ながら、現在その面影はまったくありませんが、昔この通りに大店として店を構えていた紙問屋の小津和紙を目指します。現在では移転し、こ

伝馬：馬の背に荷を積み、宿から宿へと送る制度で、江戸時代には民間の輸送に用いられた。

Around the end of the Edo Period, the **gold-silver parity** in Japan was 5 grams of silver to 1 gram of gold (1:5), which was much different from the international parity of 1:13. So, for example, if you exchanged 5 grams of silver brought into Japan from overseas for 1 gram of gold, you could then exchange that 1 gram of gold in Shanghai or Hong Kong for 13 grams of silver. And then if you exchanged those 13 grams of silver for gold in Japan, you would get nearly 3 grams of gold. In other words, you would make a nearly three-fold profit. In addition, economic chaos arose due to such problems as the confusion in money exchange because nickel silver brought in from overseas and high-valued domestic silver were exchanged on the principle of equivalence, the massive outflow of coins, and **commodity price rises**. This chaos in turn became a trigger for the Meiji Restoration.

Next, let us visit a place where evidence remains of the desperate financial straits of the Tokugawa shogunate in its closing years. Go back to Chuo-dori, head north from Mitsukoshi, and turn right at the second crossing into Odenmacho-dori. This actually was the main street of Edo in the past. In Edo times it used to be a beautiful and very bustling area with many large merchant stores, but unfortunately nowadays there are no traces of that glorious past at all. Our target is Ozu Washi, which used to be a large paper merchant on the street. The store has moved from its original site and is now located along the road, across the expressway and on the left. Founded

小津和紙
中央区日本橋本町
3-6-2
小津本館ビル
03-3662-1184
日曜定休

小津史料館（3階）
日曜定休

1653年、伊勢松坂から江戸に出てきた小津清左衛門長弘が、大伝馬町に紙商を開業。当時からの貴重な古文書などが展示されている。

の通りを進み、高速道路を横切ってすぐ左側にあります。創業1653年、幕府とも深い関係のあった**紙問屋**です。現在は紙漉き体験や色鮮やかな和紙製品の買い物などが楽しめます。

　3階にある史料館を訪れると、この紙問屋の経済人としての実力が伝わってくる珍しい展示物に出合えます。幕府へご用金として貸しつけた1万5千両、現在の価値で15億円相当の証文がガラスケースに収まっています。幕府の存続をかけての戦い、第二次長州征伐の軍事費に充てられたものです。でも、ちょっと待ってください。**証文**がまだ残っているということは？　返済は一切なし、一銭も戻らなかった証拠です。和紙は1000年の耐久性があるといわれており、消してしまいたいものも長持ちしてしまうのでご用心です。ちなみに和紙に墨で書き込んだ**大黒帳**は火事の際は井戸に投げ込まれたそうです。水にも溶けずまた乾かせば元通りになるという和紙だからこその嘘のような本当のお話です。

　最後に、小津和紙を出て左へ進み2つ目の角を左へ曲がり、1590年の徳川家康の江戸入りに同行した一代目から代々伝統を受け継いで、現在は扇子、団扇、和文具、和雑貨を扱う老舗伊場仙に立ち寄りましょう。

in 1653, this **paper wholesale merchant** had a close relationship with the Tokugawa government. Now it is possible to experience Japanese paper making and purchase colorful *washi* products here.

On the third floor there is a museum with a rare exhibit that shows just how powerful this paper wholesaler was as a business. Displayed in a glass case is a bond for 15,000 *ryo*, the equivalent of ¥1.5 billion today, lent to the Tokugawa shogunate as funding. The shogunate used the money as military spending for the Second Choshu Expedition, in which it was literally fighting for its life. But wait a minute: The fact that the **bond** remains is proof that not a penny of that loan was ever returned. Japanese paper is said to have a durability of 1,000 years, so be careful, because something you might hope will fade away will have a long life! Incidentally, when a fire broke out, people used to throw **account books** made of washi into a well. This sounds unbelievable, but apparently the ink would not dissolve in water and, when dried, the washi would return to its original state.

Finally, go out of the Ozu Washi Store, turn left, turn left again at the second corner, and you come to a famous old store called Ibasen, which handles folding fans, round fans, Japanese stationery, and Japanese sundries and has carried on traditions dating way back to 1590, when the first-generation owner of the store accompanied Tokugawa Ieyasu into Edo.

伊場仙
中央区日本橋小舟町
4-1
伊場仙ビル1階
03-3664-9261
土・日・祝日休

　伊場仙のルーツは浮世絵の版元業です。当時はかけそば1杯と同じ値段で買えた浮世絵ですが、そこに登場する絵柄は現在のグラフィックアートに匹敵する**時代の最先端をゆくもの**でした。その企画から製作、販売に至るすべてのプロデュースを担ったのが版元です。創業以来、連綿と伝統を継承してきた14代目当主は現在進行中の日本橋再開発に夢を語ります。伊場仙の洗練された江戸模様の扇子は江戸の粋そのもの。自慢できる日本橋のお土産はこれで決まりです。

Ibasen originally was a publisher of ukiyo-e woodblock prints. At that time you could buy an ukiyo-e for the same price as a bowl of noodles, but the designs that appeared were **at the forefront of the age**, rather like graphic art today. The publisher undertook all of the processes, from planning and production to sales. The current president of the company, the fourteenth-generation owner, is continuing traditions handed down since Ibasen's founding. He also has high hopes for Nihonbashi's redevelopment. Ibasen's elegant Edo-pattern folding fans are true Edo fashion and make excellent souvenirs of Nihonbashi.

Yanaka Ginza Street
谷中銀座

Yuyake Dandan
夕焼けだんだん

for Ikebukuro
池袋方面

Nippori Station
日暮里駅

Asakura Choso Museum
朝倉彫塑館

for Nishinippori
西日暮里方面

Shokichi
笑吉工房

SCAI t Bathhou
スカイ
バスハウ

JiMuSoAn
時夢草庵

Chiyoda Line
千代田線

Sendagi Station
千駄木駅

Isetatsu
いせ辰

Allan West
繪処
アラン・ウエスト

Kayaba Co
カヤバ珈

Shinobazu-dori
不忍通り

Kototoi-dori
言問通り

Nezu Station
根津駅

❶ ❷ ❸
❹ ❺ ❻

芸術香る上野から
Looking for Art:
From Ueno to Yanaka

❼

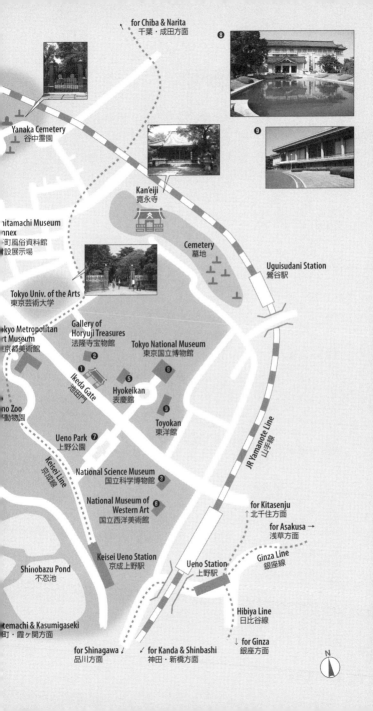

8

9

Yanaka Cemetery
谷中霊園

Kan'eiji
寛永寺

hitamachi Museum
nnex
町風俗資料館
別設展示場

Cemetery
墓地

Uguisudani Station
鶯谷駅

Tokyo Univ. of the Arts
東京芸術大学

Gallery of
Horyuji Treasures
法隆寺宝物館

Tokyo National Museum
東京国立博物館

kyo Metropolitan
t Museum
都美術館

2

Ikeda Gate
池田門

5

8

Hyokeikan
表慶館

no Zoo
動物園

9

Toyokan
東洋館

Ueno Park
上野公園
7

Keisei Line
京成線

National Science Museum
国立科学博物館
3

National Museum of
Western Art
国立西洋美術館
6

JR Yamanote Line
山手線

for Kitasenju
↑北千住方面

for Asakusa →
浅草方面

Keisei Ueno Station
京成上野駅

Ueno Station
上野駅

Ginza Line
銀座線

Shinobazu Pond
不忍池

Hibiya Line
日比谷線

temachi & Kasumigaseki
町・霞ヶ関方面

for Shinagawa ↙
品川方面

✓ for Kanda & Shinbashi
神田・新橋方面

↓ for Ginza
銀座方面

N

上野駅

日本に鉄道が敷かれたのは今から150年余り前の明治5年（1872年）、現在の新橋から横浜を目指して走る陸蒸気の出現です。その12年後、明治17年（1884年）に開業したのが上野駅です。今ではハードロックカフェ上野駅東京もある大規模な設備を誇る駅になりました。公園口改札を出るとすぐに上野公園です。近代の歴史が動き出した地、上野から現代アートの町、谷中を訪ねるルートをご紹介します。

　ここは江戸時代徳川家の菩提寺である寛永寺の30余りの伽藍があったところです。彰義隊と新政府軍の戦いですべては焼失。その後、焼け野原は近代日本の文化を象徴する博物館、美術館が集中的に設立された上野恩賜公園として生まれ変わりました。上野駅公園口を出てすぐ右側には、世界に知られるフランス人建築家ル・コルビュジェ設計の建物では日本国内に唯一現存する、国立西洋美術館があります。彼の建築の特徴として、風が吹き抜けるピロティ、自由なしかし計算された外壁面などがあります。2016年に世界文化遺産に登録された東京が誇る建物の一つを観賞し、そして、お目当ての東京国立博物館に向かいましょう。

陸蒸気：明治初期、汽車のことを総称してこう呼んだ。

ハードロックカフェ上野駅東京
台東区上野 7-1-1
アトレ上野1階
03-5826-5821
無休

彰義隊：新政府に反抗した旧幕府の家臣の集まり。2000人ほど。

国立西洋美術館
台東区上野公園7-7
050-5541-8600
毎週月曜、12月28日〜翌年1月1日 定休
（祝日が月曜の場合は開館、翌日休館）
＊2020年10月19日〜2022年春（予定）まで、全館休館中

Ueno Station

The first railway was laid in Japan more than 150 years ago, in 1872, when a **steam locomotive** operated from the present-day Shinbashi to Yokohama. Ueno Station opened 12 years later, in 1884. It is now a large station boasting many facilities, including a Hard Rock Café. If you come out through the Park Exit, Ueno Park is right in front of you. Let me guide you along the route from Ueno, the place where Japan's modern history began, to Yanaka, a community of modern art.

This is where the 30 or so buildings of Kan'eiji Temple, the **family temple** of the Tokugawa clan during the Edo Period, were located. All of them were burned down in the battle between the Shogitai, a military unit loyal to the Tokugawa shogunate and forces of the new Meiji government. Afterward, the burnt ruins were reborn as Ueno Onshi Park, where a large collection of museums and art galleries symbolizing modern Japanese culture were established. The National Museum of Western Art, the only existing building in Japan designed by the world-renowned French architect Le Corbusier, is located to the right of the Ueno Koen-guchi Exit of Ueno Station. His architecture is characterized by wind-blown pilotis and free-yet-calculated exterior surfaces. Admire one of Tokyo's most acclaimed buildings, which was registered as a World Cultural Heritage Site in 2016, and head to

東京国立博物館

東京国立博物館
台東区上野公園13-9
03-3822-1111
月曜定休
（月曜が祝日の場合は
開館、翌日休み）

　明治15年（1882年）、東京国立博物館は寛永寺本坊跡地にイギリス人ジョサイア・コンドル設計により国立の博物館として建設されました。その後関東大震災で損壊し、現在の本館が再建されたのは昭和13年（1938年）。日本最大の総合的な美術品収蔵施設として内外の**美術愛好家**でいつもにぎわっています。**国宝**89件、**重要文化財**644件を含めて12万件以上の収蔵数を誇っています。

　本館で平常陳列展示を鑑賞するだけでも2時間はたっぷりかかります。まずは中央の大階段を上がり2階からスタートします。古代から近代に至る、時代を代表する美術品が年代順に展示してあります。

　見終わって表に出ると目の前に広がる池。手前右側に堂々と立つこの博物館のシンボルツリー、ユリの木を見あげてリフレッシュしてください。博物館の生まれた時にこの地に植樹され140年、高さ24メートルの巨木です。花の形が似ていることから英語ではTulip Treeと訳されています。その右奥にあるのは、堂々とした本館とは対照的に緑のドーム屋根が

your destination, the Tokyo National Museum.

Tokyo National Museum

The Tokyo National Museum was originally constructed as a national museum on the site of the abbot's residence at Kan'eiji Temple in 1882; it was designed by the British architect Josiah Conder. The museum was damaged in the **Great Kanto Earthquake** of 1923, and the present Honkan (Japanese Gallery) was rebuilt in 1938. It is always crowded with **art enthusiasts** from Japan and abroad. The collection of more than 120,000 works of art, Japan's largest, includes 89 **National Treasures** and 644 **Important Cultural Properties**. It takes a good two hours just to see the Honkan's regular exhibition. First of all, go up the center stairway and start on the second floor. Works of art representing historical periods from ancient to modern times are displayed in chronological order.

When you go out after having viewed the museum, you'll see a pond in front of you. Refresh yourself by looking up at the museum's symbol, a magnificent lily tree standing to your right. The tree, which was planted here when the museum was built, is 140 years old and 24 meters tall. In English, it is referred to as the "Tulip Tree" because of the similarity in the shape of its flowers. To the far right is the beautiful Hyokeikan, whose central green-domed roof provides a contrast

表慶館

中央にある秀麗な建物の表慶館（ひょうけいかん）です。明治の建築家で、辰野金吾らとともに多くの大建築、たとえば、赤坂の迎賓館などを手がけた片山東熊（かたやまとうくま）の設計した建物です。入口両側に緑のライオン像のお出迎えです。よく見ると向かって左側の像は口を開け、右側の像は口を閉じています。なんとあの神社で見る"あ、うん"の一対の狛犬と同じ意匠です。建物は西洋風ですが、ピンポイントで**和様をあしらう**のがこの建築家の**真骨頂**です。

東洋館

池をはさんで反対側にはモダンな建物があります。東洋館です。日本を除く東洋の美術、工芸作品などを陳列しています。設計者は近代日本モダン建築の大御所、谷口吉郎（よしろう）です。そして彼の息子の谷口吉生（よしお）も父と同じく建築家となり、同博物館の法隆寺宝物館を設計しました。ちなみに彼は2004年11月に開館したニューヨーク近代美術館新館も設計しています。

法隆寺宝物館

法隆寺宝物館

法隆寺宝物館のファサードには全面ガラス張りの建物と大きな水盤のような池があり、そこを渡る訪問者を清々しく迎

to the imposing main building. It was designed by Tokuma Katayama, a Meiji Period architect who worked with Kingo Tatsuno and others on many major buildings, such as the State Guest House in Akasaka. You will be greeted by green lion statues on both sides of the entrance. If you look closely, you can see that the statue on the left has its mouth open and the one on the right has its mouth closed. The design is the same as that of the pair of lion-dog guardians, one with an open mouth and one with a closed mouth, that you see at shrines. The building is Western-style, but the architect has **captured Japanese style** with pinpoint accuracy, and that is the architect's **true value**.

On the other side of the pond there is a modern building. This is the Toyokan (Asian Gallery), which exhibits arts and crafts from Asian countries other than Japan. It was designed by Yoshiro Taniguchi (1904–79), a leading figure in modern Japanese architecture. Taniguchi's son, Yoshio Taniguchi, is also an architect. He designed the Gallery of Horyuji Treasures at the Tokyo National Museum and also the new Museum of Modern Art in New York, which opened in November 2004.

Gallery of Horyuji Treasures

The Horyuji Gallery has a glass façade and large pond in front of it, a refreshing welcome as visitors cross it. The collection of 300 or so items was presented

えてくれます。収蔵している300余りの収蔵物は、明治初期1878年に奈良、法隆寺から皇室に奉納されたものです。法隆寺は日本最古の寺院であり、国宝の建物、仏像、工芸品などを守ってきたのですが、明治時代になり**徳川幕府の保護**もなくなり、経済的に困窮状態に陥りました。そこで、所蔵していた国宝14点を含む319件の美術工芸品を皇室に奉納し、1万円を手にしたとのこと。現在の価値で2億円ほどです。

　古代の美術品は主に発掘されたものが多く、その出自がはっきりしていないので「**伝**」という文字がつくものが多いのですが、この宝物館が所蔵するものは法隆寺が所持していた事物というお墨付き、出所がはっきりしているという点で大変意義がありかつ価値の高いものなのです。

　展示物は7世紀からの国宝14点、重要文化財239件、8割以上が国指定文化財です。特に1階第2室の金銅仏の展示フロアは圧巻です。36体の金銅仏は1300年前の寺院内の照明レベルを再現したほの暗い中に浮かび上がります。個人の礼拝用に作った20センチほどの仏像の台座には**銘文**が読み取れるものがあります。亡くなった妻のために、あるいは子が親を偲んで作った観音菩薩があり、古代人の人間的な感情が豊かに伝わってきます。ガラスケースは窒素ガスが充填して

to the Imperial Household by Horyuji Temple in Nara in 1878, 10 years after the Meiji Restoration. Horyuji is Japan's oldest temple, and it had carefully preserved its historical buildings, Buddhist statues, and other works of art and craft. As a result of the Meiji Restoration, however, it lost the **tutelage of the Tokugawa shogunate** and fell into economic hardship. The temple therefore donated 319 works of art and craft, including 14 National Treasures, to the Imperial Household. Apparently it received ¥10,000 for them; their value today is about ¥200 million!

Ancient works of art are usually excavated, so in many cases the artist and origin are unknown. Explanations in the gallery therefore often begin with the words, "**Said to be...**" Because they clearly belonged to Horyuji, however, the works in this collection are certified and are thus extremely significant and valuable.

More than 80 percent of the works in this collection, which date from the seventh century, are cultural properties designated by the state; 14 of them are National Treasures, and 239 are Important Cultural Properties. The gilt-bronze Buddhist statues in Gallery 2 on the first floor are especially impressive. The 36 statues are displayed in semidarkness, a reproduction of the level of light that there would have been inside a temple 1,300 years ago. In some cases the sculptor's **inscription** can be seen on the pedestals of the 20-centimeter-or-so statues, which were used for private worship. There are Kannon bodhisattva statues

あり、温度が一定に保たれています。光ファイバーによる下からのひと筋の照明は古代のろうそくの明かりを再現しています。各ケースの正面には、よくある名称や解説の札が見当たりません。そこには、**先入観念**のないまま、まずは鑑賞し、味わい、仏像と対峙してほしいという本館の意図があります。ケースの周囲をぐるりと見てください。横に解説がついています。近づいて見ると仏像の横や後ろにも精巧な装飾が施されているのがわかります。

観音菩薩とは、真理に目覚めて如来になる一歩手前で、いまだ修行中の仏様です。慈悲深く、この世で苦しみ悩んでいる人がすべて救われることを誓願しています。ところで仏像の種類を見分ける簡単な方法をご紹介しましょう。それは衣服や装飾品を見ればすぐ分かります。

悟りを開いた如来は飾り気のない1枚の法衣だけを身につけます。頭部にも何もつけないことがほとんどです。次に菩薩は仏教の創始者である釈迦族のゴータマ・シッダールタが王子だった頃の衣服や装飾品を身につけています。ネックレスや長く垂らした髪、肩から流れるように巻かれたスカーフなど、美しく飾りたてられています。特に千手観音菩薩はあ

for a husband in memory of a deceased wife or for children in memory of their parents. They amply convey the human sentiments of ancient people. The glass cases are filled with nitrogen gas, and the temperature is kept at a certain level. Optic-fiber lighting from below reproduces the candlelight of ancient times. The cases do not have the usual tags on their fronts giving the name of the work and an explanation. The desire of the gallery is to have visitors first of all look at the statues without any **preconceived ideas**, savoring them and confronting them. Look round the cases, and you will find the explanations on the sides. When you look closely, you will notice that the statues are elaborately decorated on the sides and behind as well.

The Kannon bodhisattva is a being that refrains from entering nirvana in order to compassionately help others who are suffering in the world. By the way, do you know how to distinguish between the different types of Buddhist statue? There is a simple method: Just look at the clothing and accessories, and you will soon understand.

First of all, a being that has achieved enlightenment and **entered nirvana** is austere and wears just a single robe. In most cases they do not have anything on their heads. Next, the bodhisattva wears the clothing and accessories that Sakyamuni (also known as Gautama Siddhartha), the founder of Buddhism, wore when he was a prince. This includes a necklace, long dangling hair, and a scarf flowing from the neck. In particular, the Thousand-armed Kannon bodhisattva changes

らゆる人々を救うために変幻自在に姿を変えるのです。頭の上ににぎやかに11面の小さい顔をのせ、さまざまな道具を持った千本の手を差し伸べていたりします。超能力の持ち主であり、その能力を多次元で表現しています。

そのほか明王や天部と呼ばれる仏像があります。如来や菩薩の穏やかな表情とまるで違う、はっきりした**人間的感情**が表れています。明王は目をむいた怒った表情です。如来や菩薩の言うことを聞かない愚かな人々を烈火のごとく怒り、反省してやり直せと励ましています。最後の天部は仏教を悪霊や邪気から守るガードマンです。宮廷で仕えていた女官の姿をしている吉祥天や弁才天は女性的なやさしい姿ですが、ほかは戦士のように鎧をまとったものなど戦闘モードそのものです。

さて法隆寺宝物館ではほかにも、教科書でよく見かける、お釈迦様が、母である摩耶夫人の袖口から誕生するその瞬間を造形化した「摩耶夫人及び天人像」も見逃せません。また、国宝の水瓶は**名品中の名品**です。竜の頭を注ぎ口、身体を把手にかたどり、胴部分には**ササン朝ペルシャ**の天馬ペガサス文様が見られます。東の竜と西の天馬がシルクロードを行きかい、ひとつの水瓶にみごとに共存し、美しくよみがえったのです。

竜首水瓶：飛鳥時代の作品とされる。

appearance freely in order to help all kinds of people. The image has 11 small faces on top of its head and a thousand arms holding various instruments. It has supernatural powers and expresses them in many dimensions.

There are also Buddhist statues called Myo-o (wisdom kings) and Tenbu (heavenly guardians). In contrast to the serene expressions of the Buddha and bodhisattva images, these images express vivid **human sentiments**. Myo-o have furious and glaring expressions. They are angry at the foolish people who do not listen to the words of the Buddha or the bodhisattva and implore them to do some soul searching and mend their ways. Tenbu are guardsmen, protecting Buddhism from evil spirits and malice. Kichijoten and Benzaiten are gentle feminine figures in the form of court ladies, but Myo-o and Tenbu are like warriors, clad in armor and ready to fight.

In the Gallery of Horyuji Treasures you also should not miss the sculpture *Lady Maya and Three Heavenly Beings*, which depicts the moment when Sakyamuni is born from the sleeve of his mother, Queen Maya, a story that is often told in textbooks. And the **crème de la crème** is the *Dragonhead Pitcher*, a water jar that is designated a National Treasure. Its spout and handle imitate the head and body of a dragon, respectively, while the body of the pitcher has the pattern of the flying horse Pegasus of the **Persian Sassanid dynasty** (third to seventh

寛永寺

池田屋敷表門：現在
の鳥取県、因州池田家
の表門。屋敷門として
は国持大名の格式を
持っており、国の重要
文化財となっている。

唐破風屋根：屋根の
上半分をふくらませ、
下半分に反りをつけた
装飾性の高い豪奢な
屋根。

東京国立博物館の正面の門を出て右へ
進むと、旧池田家屋敷の表門がどっしり
と建っています。もともと丸の内にあっ
た屋敷の正門が東宮御所、高松宮邸と移
築を重ね、最終的に現在の地に落ち着き
ました。大屋根の下に２つの**唐破風屋根**
があり、当時の大名の威光が伝わる立派
な門です。

この門を通り過ぎて国立博物館の敷地
の角を右へ曲がり、東京芸術大学のキャ
ンパスを左に見ながら進みます。ほどな
くすると静かな住宅街の右手に、白い壁
に囲まれた大きな本堂の偉容が見えてき
ます。江戸時代、奈良の東大寺と同じ規
模の建造物を有していたともいわれる上
野寛永寺の現代の姿です。広大な敷地を
誇っていた寛永寺は江戸時代、仏教寺院
の最高位にあった寺のひとつでした。

寛永寺は江戸城に対して北の方角にあ
る小高い台地に建てられました。悪霊が
攻め入るのは北東の鬼門からです。京都

寛永寺
台東区上野桜木
1-14-11

centuries). The dragon of the East and the flying horse of the West crossed the Silk Road, came together in a single pitcher, and were beautifully reborn.

Kan'eiji Temple

Going out of the main entrance to the Tokyo National Museum, turn right, and you come to the stately front gate of the former Ikeda family residence. Originally this gate stood in front of a mansion in Marunouchi; it reached its present site via Togu Palace and the residence of Prince Takamatsu. Under the large roof there are two **hip-gabled roofs** over guardhouses. It is a splendid gate that fully conveys the power of the daimyo in the Edo Period.

Go past this gate, turn right at the corner with the precincts of the Tokyo National Museum on the right, and walk straight ahead, taking a look at the Tokyo University of the Arts campus on your left as you proceed. Eventually, on the right side of a quiet residential district, a splendid temple building surrounded by a white wall will come into view. This is Ueno Kan'eiji Temple, which during the Edo Period is said to have been as large as Todaiji Temple in Nara. Kan'eiji was one of Japan's most important Buddhist temples at that time.

Kan'eiji Temple was built on a hill to the north of Edo Castle, because it was believed that evil spirits would attack from the northeast. Just as Kyoto was

の北東には比叡山の延暦寺、江戸の北東には上野の寛永寺がそれぞれの都を守っていました。徳川家の繁栄祈願と**菩提を弔う**お寺でもあります。

徳川家初代将軍家康は死後、自らが造った都、江戸を見守りながら、遠く天皇の住む京都に睨みをきかせるために東の方角で照り輝く神様、東照大権現となりました。後に世界遺産に登録されることになる日光東照宮に**神として奉られた**わけです。

東照大権現：1616年家康没の翌年、後水尾天皇から家康に贈られた称号。

絢爛豪華なお宮は世界中の訪問者を魅了しています。「日光を見ずして結構と言うなかれ」。ニッコウとケッコウは韻を踏んでいるので、海外からのお客様にはこのことわざがうけます。

そして残りの将軍たちは**西方極楽浄土**で仏様になるべく祭られました。日本を265年間統治した徳川ファミリーは今でも健在ですが、江戸時代を支配したのは15人の将軍です。初代家康と3代家光はそれぞれ日光の東照宮と輪王寺大猷院、2代目秀忠を含む6名は港区芝の増上寺、5代目綱吉を含む6名が上野寛永寺に祭られました。**仏教と神道が共存する**日本ならではの寛容でおおらかな宗教観といえるでしょう。

guarded by Enryakuji Temple on Mount Hiei, in the northeastern part of the city, so Edo was protected by Kan'eiji in the northeast. It was also the family temple of the Tokugawa clan, praying for the prosperity and **repose of family members**.

After his death, the first Tokugawa shogun, Ieyasu (1543–1616), was canonized under the title of Tosho Daigongen, a deity shining in the direction of the east, guarding Edo, the capital that he himself had created, and exerting his authority over distant Kyoto, where the emperor resided. Ieyasu was **enshrined as a deity** at Toshogu Shrine in Nikko, which is now registered as a World Heritage Site.

This dazzling shrine fascinates visitors from around the world. There is a saying in Japanese that goes, "Never say *kekko* until you see Nikko." Even foreigners who do not know any Japanese like this proverb, because kekko, which means "splendid," rhymes with Nikko.

The other shoguns, by the way, were enshrined so that their souls might rest in peace in the **Western Paradise of Buddha**. The Tokugawa family, which still survives today, produced 15 shoguns, who controlled Japan for 265 years during the Edo Period. The first shogun, Ieyasu, and the third, Iemitsu, were buried in Nikko, at Toshogu Shrine and Daiyuin of Rinnoji Temple, respectively. Six others, including the second, Hidetada, were buried at Zojoji Temple in Shiba, Tokyo, and six more, including the fifth, Tsunayoshi, were interred at Kan'eiji. This **coexistence of Shinto and Buddhism** is typical of the tolerant

現代でも我々は現世利益を求めて神様がいらっしゃる神社へ、**来世利益**はお寺で仏様に拝みます。人生の節目の儀式を巧みにより分けて神社や寺院を訪れます。キリスト教による結婚式もしています。外国人への説明では、「生まれたときは神道、結婚式はクリスチャン、そしてお葬式は仏式で」などと言っています。あまりにも不謹慎、不道徳と誤解を受けないように、補足しながら説明してみましょう。一人の神を信奉するのではなく、**土着の宗教**と、キリスト教や仏教のように国境を越えて世界的に広まった宗教を共存させて、**多様な宗教文化**を作り上げるのはアジア人の得意とするところです。いいとこ取りではなく、異文化を理解し、受け入れ、共生させ、より成熟したものにしてきたのです。日本の宗教観、自信をもって紹介したいものです。

閑話休題、寛永寺の**境内**へ入りましょう。川越から移築された本堂の裏側、隣接する学校の校舎との間に門があります。その門をくぐると、国立博物館の裏塀とJRの線路にはさまれるように広がる寛永寺の墓所があります。訪れる人は少ないのですが、落ち着いた、きれいに手入れが行き届いた霊園です。

ここに6人の将軍を祭る宝塔や廟（びょう）があります。しばし歴史的人物達の終（つい）の棲家（すみか）

寛永寺：寛永2 (1625) 年、天海が開山、天台宗。

and open-minded view of religion in Japan.

Even today, the Japanese go to Shinto shrines to pray for matters that concern their interests in the present world and to Buddhist temples to pray for matters that concern their **interests in the next world**. The Japanese visit shrines to fete certain milestones in life and temples to mark others. Church weddings are popular, too. I explain to foreigners that "We are born as Shintoists, get married as Christians, and die as Buddhists." But this might sound imprudent and unethical and be misunderstood, so it should be added that rather than believing in one god, Asian people are good at mixing **indigenous beliefs** with religions that have gone beyond national borders and spread worldwide, such as Christianity and Buddhism, thereby creating **diverse religious cultures**. The Japanese have not just taken in what they thought was good; they have understood different cultures and accepted, absorbed, and adapted them. We Japanese must explain Japan's religious views with confidence.

To return to our subject, let's enter the **precincts** of Kan'eiji. Go through the gate that stands between the main hall, which was moved here from Kawagoe, and a school adjacent to it. When you enter, you will see the large cemetery of Kan'eiji, as if sandwiched between the outer wall of the Tokyo National Museum and the JR railway lines. There are few visitors, but it is a very tranquil and well-kept cemetery.

Six shoguns are interred here, in bronze, tower-like graves and mausoleums. How about spending a

に身を置くのはいかがでしょうか。江戸時代265年間、戦いもなく、鎖国制度を守りつつ、**自給自足社会**を存続させた徳川将軍家の偉業にふさわしい立派な墓所ですが、残念ながら将軍たちが祭られている宝塔が並ぶところは高い石塀に囲まれていてよく見ることはできません。入り口の門の隙間から眺めると、高い杉の木に守られるように置かれた宝塔は日光東照宮にある家康が眠る宝塔とほぼ同じ大きさであることが分かります。自由に入れるのは上野のカラスだけです。

谷中霊園

　残る一人、ラストショーグン徳川慶喜のお墓が気になります。徳川家の菩提寺であった寛永寺の奥の一室で**謹慎**し、江戸城と徳川家の最後を見定めた後、水戸、静岡と居を移し、明治時代まで公爵として最後の日々を送った慶喜でした。彼は寛永寺から言問通りをへだてた北側にある緑あふれる東京の桜の名所のひとつ、谷中霊園の中に祀られました。

谷中霊園
台東区谷中7-5-24
03-3821-4456
（管理所）

　谷中霊園はJR日暮里駅にほぼ隣接し、上野公園からも15分程度あれば到着します。上野の丘には北に寛永寺、西に天

moment at this final resting place of these historical figures? It is a splendid cemetery worthy of the Tokugawa Shoguns, who, without armed conflict, maintained a policy of national isolation, and created a **self-sufficient society** for 265 years during the Edo Period. Unfortunately, the part of the cemetery with the monuments to the shoguns is surrounded by a high wall and cannot be seen very well. Peering through a gap in the entrance, you can see that the monuments, which seem to be protected by large cedars, are about the same size as that of Ieyasu at Toshogu Shrine in Nikko. Only the Ueno crows can enter freely.

Yanaka Cemetery

One wonders where the grave of the Last Shogun, Tokugawa Yoshinobu, might be. Well, after **being confined in** a room at the back of Kan'eiji, the Tokugawa family temple, and confirming the fall of Edo Castle and the end of the Tokugawa Era, Yoshinobu moved to Mito and Shizuoka and spent his final years, during the Meiji Period, as a duke. He is buried at the verdant Yanaka Cemetery, which is just to the north of Kan'eiji, on the other side of Kototoi-dori. This is also one of Tokyo's most popular spots for cherry-blossom viewing.

Yanaka Cemetery is nearly adjacent to JR Nippori Station, and is only about 15 minutes from Ueno Park. On Ueno's hill, Kan'eiji Temple was to the north and

王寺があり、明治になった時、二つの寺の間に東京の市民のために造営されました。**宗派や階級も問わない**、新しい時代を思わせる、東京都が今も管理する霊園です。谷中霊園には一部寛永寺の墓地もあり、そこにラストショーグンは眠っています。

それでは、言問通りを横切って彼のお墓を目指します。50メートルほど進んで、左側に白い道標「乙10号11側」と小さな石の案内があります。そこを左へ曲がり、さらに次の案内板に沿って右へ曲がると、目の前に**三つ葉葵の御紋**がついた門があります。やっと江戸時代の終焉（しゅうえん）の地にたどりついた感があります。中には入れませんが、低い塀と門の格子の間から2つの円墳が見えます。向かって右側が慶喜、左はその奥方のものです。

徳川慶喜の墓

明治維新で活躍したほかのすべてのサムライ達、そして、明治天皇も既に他界し、一人残ったラストショーグンは77歳で亡くなります。政治の表舞台から身を引き、しかし、公爵の立場で亡くなりました。趣味を生かして、生まれ変わった日本の残したい風景、市井の人々らの写真を多く撮影して残し、静岡の**殖産事業**へも貢献し、見事な生きざまでした。サムライは日本から完全にいなくなりましたが、ラストショーグンは生き残り、悠々自適に長寿を全うしました。

Tennoji Temple to the west. When the Meiji Period came, the cemetery was built between the two temples for citizens of Tokyo. The cemetery is still managed by the Tokyo Metropolitan Government, and as befits the new era, there **no distinctions of religious sect or social class**. The Yanaka Cemetery also contains the cemetery of Kan'eiji Temple, where the Last Shogun rests.

Let's cross Kototoi-dori Avenue to get to his grave. About 50 meters on, there is a signpost with the characters "乙10号11側" and a small stone giving directions on the left. Turn left here and then, following the information board ahead, right. In front of you there is a gate with a **crest of three hollyhock leaves**. Welcome to the place where the Edo Period came to a definite end. You cannot go inside, but between the low wall and the gate you can see two burial mounds. Yoshinobu is on your right, his wife on the left.

All the other samurai who participated in the Meiji Restoration, as well as the Emperor Meiji, have already passed away, and the remaining "Last Shogun" dies at the age of 77. He withdrew from the political scene, but died with the title of prince. He made the most of his hobby, taking and preserving many photographs of the scenery and people of the reborn Japan, and also contributed to Shizuoka's **industrial development project**. Samurai have completely disappeared from Japan, but the Last Shogun survived and lived a long and comfortable life.

谷中のアートロード

谷中霊園から言問通りに戻り、右へ進むとほどなく右側に旧吉田屋酒店、現在は下町風俗資料館付設展示場があります。店の中に入るとほぼ**100年前にタイムスリップした**かのようです。1910年に建てられた建物をそのまま保存し、公開しています。**当時のようすがわかる**商売道具が満載です。酒樽はもちろん、砂糖、塩、米などを入れるガラス扉のついた棚台があります。マイボトルを持って必要な調味料を**測り売り**で買っていたエコな日本人の生活ぶりに感心します。木製のシャッターで柱も移動式、必要な時に、間口を大きくあけ荷車を奥まで入れたり出したりしていた当時の人の知恵も見事です。

下町風俗資料館付設展示場
台東区上野桜木2-10-6
03-3823-4408
月曜定休
(祝日が月曜の場合は開館、翌日休み)

吉田屋：谷中6丁目で江戸時代から代々酒屋を営んできた。建物は出桁造りで、明治時代の商家の特徴がよく見られる。

旧吉田屋酒店の眼の前にあるカヤバ珈琲は、80年ほど前に創業したおしゃれなカフェです。この角から谷中の魅力であるアートギャラリー、カフェ、骨董品、陶磁器、民芸小物店などが並ぶ散歩道が始まります。

3分ほど歩いて右側にある「上野桜木あたり」に立ち寄って、小休憩をとるのがおすすめ。古民家3棟を改装した**複合施設**です。多種のビールが楽しめる"谷

カヤバ珈琲
台東区谷中6-1-29
03-5832-9896
月曜定休

Yanaka Art Road

Returning to Kototoi-dori from Yanaka Cemetery, turn right and you will soon find the former Yoshida-ya Liquor Store on your right, which is now an exhibition space attached to the Shitamachi Museum. Enter the building, and you will feel as if you **have traveled back in time a hundred years**. The building, built in 1910, has been preserved and is open to the public. It's filled with equipment used in the liquor store that shows **how things were done back then**. In addition to sake barrels, there are shelving units with glass doors for storing sugar, salt, rice, and other items. The eco-friendly lifestyle of people who brought their own bottles to purchase seasoning that was **sold in measured amounts** is admirable, and the pillars could be moved using wooden shutters so that the entranceway could be enlarged to allow carts into the back, show the intelligence of people back then.

Kayaba Coffee, located right in front of the old Yoshida-ya liquor store, is a stylish café that was established about 80 years ago. A pedestrian path lined with art galleries, cafés, antiques, ceramics, and folk art stores that express Yanaka's charm begins at this corner.

Walk three minutes, and then I recommend stopping by Ueno Sakuragi Atari on the right to take a short break. It is a **complex** of three old houses that have been renovated. You can enjoy a variety of beers

中ビアホール"、アルコールが苦手な方は、VANERでパンとコーヒーをお供にひととき過ごしてみてください。このネーミングは不思議ですが、上野桜木あたり、そのまままさに、この地区の住所です。

　元の道に戻って進むと、次のスポットは左側の200年前の銭湯を改築した現代アートギャラリー「スカイザバスハウス」。昼からオープンしています。お風呂は市民の一番の楽しみであり、**社交場と**して建物は豪華に作られました。当時は壁には必ず**富士山の雄姿**が描かれていたのですが、そこを現代アートを楽しむ場にする発想はさすが。谷中はこのあたりから不忍通りに向かって何本かの坂道が迷路のように交差して広がり、70余りの寺院がある寺町が原点の町です。

　昔の銭湯の立派な建物の入口からそのまままっすぐ進み、白い塀に囲まれたお寺ばかりの路地になったら、遠方にひときわ大きな一本のヒマラヤ杉が見えてきます。そこに向かってゆくとアメリカ人画家アラン・ウエスト氏のアトリエ兼画廊が左にあります。一歩踏み込むと正面にまるで小劇場の舞台のように制作場が設けてあり、アラン氏が江戸時代の絵師さながらにお出迎えをしてくれます。展示された作品の鑑賞だけでなく、制作工程や画材の説明もきっと快くしてくれるはずです。大小の和筆で描かれた屏風絵

SCAI THE
BATHHOUSE
台東区谷中6-1-23
柏湯跡
03-3821-1144
日・月・祝日 定休

繪処アラン・ウエスト
台東区谷中1-6-17
03-3827-1907

at the Yanaka Beer Hall, and if you don't like alcohol, spend a few minutes trying the bread and coffee at Vaner. The name, which means "Ueno Sakuragi vicinity," may sound strange, but it comes from the actual address of this area.

Back on the original route, the next spot on the left is SCAI the Bathhouse, a contemporary art gallery housed in a 200-year-old public bath. It is open from noon. Going to public baths was once the most popular pastime for local citizens, and the building was luxuriously constructed as a **social gathering place**. In those days, the walls were always painted with the **majestic image of Mt. Fuji**, and it was a great idea to turn it into a place to enjoy contemporary art. This is the starting point of Yanaka's temple area, where more than 70 temples spread out like a maze from here to Shinobazu Street.

From the entrance of a magnificent old public bath building, go straight ahead, and when you reach an alley full of temples surrounded by white walls, you will see a large Himalayan cedar in the distance. Walk toward that tree, and the studio and gallery of Allan West, an American folding screen artist, appears on the left. One step inside immediately reveals a workshop looking for all the world like a small theater setting. Mr. West, like a Edo-period painter, comes out to greet you. Apart from enjoying the works on display, you will undoubtedly be treated to an explanation of the materials and processes that produced the art. The screens and hanging scrolls

や掛け軸は**金箔や銀箔**が施され、光のあたり具合で美しさが引き立つ色彩豊かな作品です。また、このアトリエで年に2回ほど「絵処能」と題して能楽公演も開かれています。**屏風絵**と能楽の融合はアラン氏の存在があって生まれた稀有な芸術空間です。制作時間は夕方から夜中なので、アトリエは午後から開きます。訪問前に電話での確認をおすすめします。

次に少し戻って先ほどの細い道を進み、長久院の前の路地を入ると谷中の墨絵画家ジム・ハサウェイ氏のアトリエ時夢草庵です。細い路地をこよなく愛するジムさんのアトリエの入り口には墨絵で描かれた看板。ひょっとしたら墨絵の作品を見せてもらえるかもしれません。

ジム・ハサウェイ時夢草庵
台東区谷中4-1-16
090-1842-1612

ジム・ハサウェイ氏

are all painted with Japanese brushes of various sizes and make use of **gold and silver leaf**, which according to the lighting brings out the rich coloring of these striking works. Twice a year at this studio a performance of Noh called Court Atelier Noh is performed. It is a remarkable merging of Noh and **folding screen** art that owes its existence entirely to Allan West. Production hours are from evening to night, so the studio opens in the afternoon. It is recommended to call and check before visiting.

Walk back to the narrow road and keep going along it until you reach Chokyuin temple. Enter the alley in front of this temple and you come to JiMuSoAn, the studio of the American *sumi-e* (ink painting) artist Jim Hathaway, who is very fond of the alleys in this area. In front of the studio there is a signboard written in sumi-e. If you are lucky, Jim might show you some of his paintings.

朝倉彫塑館

　さらに北へ進むと少し広めの通りに出ます。台東初音幼稚園に突き当たったらそこを右へ折れます。ひとつ目の角から、また細い道を左に進んでください。一方通行の道は向かってくる車に注意して歩きます。5分ほど歩いた右手に、特徴ある塀で囲まれた朝倉彫塑館があります。

　東洋のロダンと称せられた近代彫刻家、朝倉文夫のアトリエ兼住居は、8年の歳月をかけて1935年に完成した鉄筋コンクリートと日本建築が繋がっている建物です。5年にわたる耐震補強改装工事が2013年秋に完了し、以前と全く変わらない**外観、内部意匠**が復活しました。入口で靴を脱ぎ、まずは3階まで吹き抜けのアトリエ棟で**代表作**である「墓守」などを鑑賞し、廊下で繋がっている住居部分の各部屋のデザインや調度品を観賞します。

朝倉彫塑館
台東区谷中7-18-10
03-3821-4549
月・木曜 定休（祝日
と重なる場合は開館、
翌日休館）

Asakura Museum of Sculpture

Keep going north and you come to a slightly wider road. When you reach Taito Hatsune Kindergarten, turn right, and then turn left at the first corner into a narrower lane. This is a one-way street, so beware of the cars coming toward you. After about five minutes you will see the Asakura Choso Memorial Museum on your right, surrounded by a distinctive wall.

This was the studio and house of the modern sculptor Fumio Asakura (1883–1964), who was known as the "Rodin of the East." The original buildings, which were completed in 1935 after eight years of work, were a combination of ferroconcrete and traditional Japanese domestic architecture. In autumn 2013, a five-year-long renovation of the museum to make it earthquake resistant was completed, and the **outer appearance and interior design** were restored to their original condition. After removing your shoes at the entrance, you go up to the third floor atelier with atrium and take in Asakura's **representative works**, including the Grave Guardian, then go via a connecting corridor to the living area and its individual rooms, each with its own delightful design and furnishings.

また庭の方に目を向けると、驚くこと
に中庭一面が井戸水を利用した池になっ
ています。その池に配置された大小の5
つの岩に注目です。それぞれ**仁、義、礼、
智、信**の儒教の教えを表しているとのこ
と。自己の精神のあり方を反省、見直す
ための意匠だそうです。池を取り囲むよ
うに茶室や居間が建てられています。本
来ならそれぞれの部屋の座敷に座って水
のお庭をゆっくり眺め、静謐（せいひつ）な時間を満
喫したいところです。

　ここで外国人を日本建築にお連れする
際に覚えておきたいことをひとつ。身長
の高い外国人や若者が日本建築を訪れる
と**鴨居（かもい）**に頭をぶつけたり、天井が低く圧
迫感を感じます。そのため本来の日本間
の美しさに気がつかないかも知れませ
ん。日本建築は**座敷に座ったときの目線**
を意識してすべてがデザインされている
のです。庭を眺めるときももちろん座敷
に座るようにします。そうして**障子**を開
けると、**鴨居**と**敷居**、両側の障子で区切
られた庭の景色はまさに一幅の絵となり
ます。
　最後にアトリエ棟の屋上庭園を訪ねて
みてください。朝倉氏の園芸への造詣の
深さが感じられる植栽が見られます。屋
上をかざる彫刻にもご注目ください。ひ

When you look into the garden, you will notice that, surprisingly, the small courtyard is occupied by a pond that uses well water. Note the five stones of varying sizes in the pond. They represent the five Confucian virtues of **benevolence, justice, courtesy, wisdom, and sincerity**. Apparently Asakura came up with this design to reflect on and amend his own thinking. A tea ceremony room and living room encircle the pond. Under normal circumstances, visitors would be able to enjoy a very peaceful moment, sitting in those rooms and gazing at the water. For the time being, though, you will just have to imagine the serenity.

There is one thing that I want you to remember when showing Japanese architecture to foreigners. When they visit Japanese homes, tall foreigners often bang their heads on the **lintels** and complain that the low ceilings make them feel oppressed. For that reason, sometimes they do not appreciate the essential beauty of a Japanese-style room. Japanese architecture is designed from the **perspective of someone sitting on the tatami-mat floor**. And people should be seated when they look out into the garden, too. Then open **sliding door**, and the view of the garden framed by the lintel, the **sill**, and the sliding doors on both sides really does make a picture.

Finally, you should visit the garden on the roof above the atelier. Here you can see various kinds of plant life that show the depth of Asakura's understanding of gardening. You should pay

とつは若々しい砲丸投げの選手の像、そして、もうひとつは、ラングドン・ウォーナー博士の胸像です。アメリカ人の東洋美術史家です。諸説ありますが、第二次世界大戦のとき、京都など**爆撃すべきでない都市のリスト**を作成しアメリカ政府へ進言したとされています。感謝の意を込めて終戦直後、博士の胸像や碑が京都や鎌倉でも建てられました。博士の視線の先には東京スカイツリーが遠望できます。日本の伝統美を救ったとされる博士の目にはどのように映っているのでしょう。

谷中銀座

　アートに触れる散策もそろそろお腹がすいてくる時間となりました。朝倉彫塑館を出て、先ほどの道をそのまま進み、突き当たって左へ曲がると目の前に広い階段です。ここから夕焼けが階段の先の空に見えるので「夕焼けだんだん」と呼ばれています。階段を下りてゆくと一気に夕食の買い物でにぎわう商店街、谷中銀座です。揚げたてのさつま揚げ、できたてのお団子、お惣菜、おせんべいとすべて買って帰りたくなるものばかり。**誘惑と戦いながら**、沈む夕陽に照らされて谷中の小旅行を終わりにしましょう。

夕焼けだんだん

particular attention to the sculpture displayed on the roof. One is the statue of a youthful shot-putter; the other is a bust of Dr. Langdon Warner. Dr. Warner was an American art historian specializing in East Asian art. According to some, it was he who advised the American government to include Kyoto on the **list of Japanese cities not to be bombed** during the World War II. In the postwar period, monuments and busts of Langdon were erected in Kyoto and Kamakura for this reason. The rooftop bust is looking out toward Tokyo Skytree. What would the man who is said to have saved Japanese traditional art think of this colossal structure.

Yanaka Ginza

Having savored so much art, you must be feeling hungry by now. Go out of the Asakura Choso Memorial Museum, keep going along the road that you came in by, and turn left at the end. You will see some wide steps in front of you. This is called the Yuyake Dandan ("sunset terrace"), because beautiful sunsets can be seen from here. Go down the steps, and the atmosphere changes completely. You are on Yanaka Ginza Street, where crowds of people are doing their last-minute shopping for the evening meal. Freshly fried fish-paste loaf, freshly made dumplings, side dishes, rice crackers — the delights are sure to make your mouth water. **Battling temptation**, let's

いせ辰
台東区谷中2-18-9
03-3823-1453
元旦のみ休み

笑吉工房
台東区谷中3-2-6
03-3821-1837
月、火曜定休 (祝日開館)

　時間に余裕があれば、谷中銀座から不忍通りに出てください。千代田線千駄木駅を目指して進み団子坂交差点を左に折れて坂を少し上がったところ、右側に和紙のいせ辰谷中店、手前左側のそば屋の隣には指人形店笑吉工房があります。ご主人手作りの穏やかに微笑む人形が、今日の散策の疲れた足腰と心を癒してくれます。3人以上なら30分の人形パフォーマンスがいつでも楽しめます（大人一人500円）。大笑い、苦笑いの絶妙人形劇です。写真を持参すれば5か月ほどかかりますが、似顔絵指人形も作ってくれます。驚きのプレゼントになるかも。笑顔の人形に笑顔で応え、帰路につきましょう。

　ところで、この界隈は月曜日に休む店や施設が多いのですが、なぜかと言うと、この地区の文化・芸術を支えている東京公立博物館が月曜休館のためです。**思わず納得**です。

谷中銀座

end out tour of Yanaka here, as the sun goes down.

If you do still have a little time and energy to spare, walk from Yanaka Ginza onto Shinobazu-dori and head in the direction of Sendagi Station on the Chiyoda subway line. Turn left at the Dangozaka ("dumpling hill") crossing, walk up the hill a little, and you come to the Yanaka store of Isetatsu, which specializes in *washi* (Japanese paper), on the right, and on the left, next to a soba restaurant, the Shokichi hand-puppet shop. The gentle smiles of the owner's hand-made puppets are sure to soothe you after today's long walk. If you make a reservation beforehand, you can watch a 30-minute performance at any time (500 yen for adults). Each performance is chockfull of laughter and drollery. It takes five months to complete, but if you take along a picture of yourself, the shop will make a finger puppet resembling you. This might make an unusual present for someone. In any case, matching the smiles of the puppets, put a smile on your face as you bring the day to a close.

By the way, many stores and facilities in this neighborhood are closed on Mondays because the Tokyo Public Museum, which supports the culture and art of this area, is closed on Mondays. **It makes sense to me.**

気品あふれる銀座から

Still as Posh as Ever: Ginza

for Yurakucho & Ikebukuro
有楽町・池袋方面

JR Yamanote Line
山手線

Yurakucho Station
有楽町駅

for Roppongi & Nakameguro
六本木・中目黒方面

Yurakucho Mallion
有楽町マリオン

for Yotsuya & Shinjuku
四谷・新宿方面

GINZA 5 FIVE
銀座ファイブ

Seiyudo
誠友堂

Ginza S
銀座駅

Hyakunin Isshu
百人一趣

Marunouchi Line
丸の内線

Harum
晴海通

for Shinbashi
新橋方面

Shiseido Parlor
資生堂パーラー

Chuo-dori
中央通

Ginza Line
銀座線

for Shinbashi & Shibuya
新橋・渋谷方面

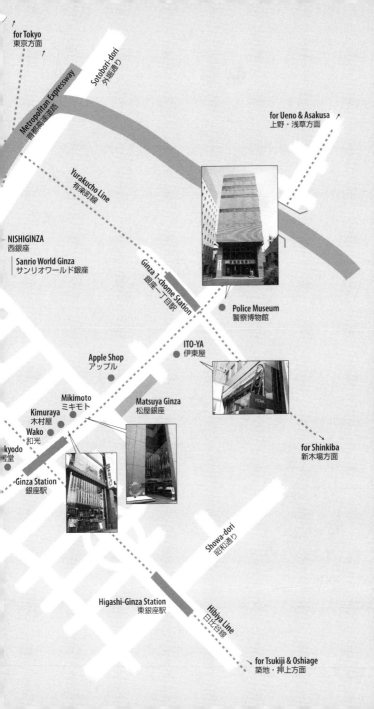

for Tokyo
東京方面

Sotobori-dori
外堀通り

Metropolitan Expressway
首都高速道路

for Ueno & Asakusa
上野・浅草方面

Yurakucho Line
有楽町線

NISHIGINZA
西銀座

Sanrio World Ginza
サンリオワールド銀座

Ginza 1-chome Station
銀座一丁目駅

Police Museum
警察博物館

ITO-YA
伊東屋

Apple Shop
アップル

Mikimoto
ミキモト

Matsuya Ginza
松屋銀座

Kimuraya
木村屋

Wako
和光

kyodo
号堂

for Shinkiba
新木場方面

Ginza Station
銀座駅

Showa-dori
昭和通り

Higashi-Ginza Station
東銀座駅

Hibiya Line
日比谷線

for Tsukiji & Oshiage
築地・押上方面

銀座

銀貨鋳造所：初め江戸幕府は、大阪、長崎など4カ所に設置したが、不正事件が起きたため、江戸1カ所に置いた。1869年に造幣局が設置されるまで、銀貨の鋳造、発行を行った。

　銀座は、かつて徳川幕府の**銀貨鋳造所**が置かれ、銀の座があったことがその名の由来です。明治時代になって、1872年に起こった大火で、銀座一帯の建物は消失。そして日本初の煉瓦街が代わりに登場しました。アイルランド人**お雇い建築家**トーマス・ジェームズ・ウォートルスの設計はまるで西洋風長屋で、両側に続く2階建て煉瓦造りの商業施設と住宅がずらりと並んでいました。日本で初めて、歩道が設けられ、ガス灯が灯り、柳が風にそよぎ、レンガ造りの店が立ち並ぶ西洋風の街並みです。一直線に伸びる800メートルにおよぶ通りには**目障りな電線**や突き出した看板がなく、歩道の幅の広さが伸びやかさを醸し出します。

　高速道路がまたがる銀座1丁目の角には警察博物館。もし追いかけられたら身も心も縮む思いの白バイですが、その白バイにまたがっての記念写真はいかがでしょうか。そして、ここから銀座通りのガイドが始まります。

　銀座の街の創設にあたっては、3つのコンセプトがあったそうです。西欧文化のよさを味わいつつ、最先端をいく商品の買い物のできる街に、訪日する外国人に対して立派な商店街で日本の近代化をア

警察博物館
中央区京橋3-5-1
03-3581-4321
月曜休館（祝日の場合は開館、翌日休館）
入館無料　予約優先

Ginza

In the Edo Period the Tokugawa shogunate used to have a **mint for casting silver coins** in the Ginza area, and that is where the name comes from: "Ginza" means "silver mint." During the Meiji Period, the buildings of the Ginza district were destroyed in the great fire of 1872. However, after that they were replaced by Japan's first district filled with brick buildings. Designed by Thomas James Waters, an Irish **architect for hire**, they resembled Western-style row houses. The two-story brick structures ran in rows along both sides of the street, and there were both commercial and residential buildings. Today the straight, 800-meter street does not have any **unsightly power lines** or protrusive signboards, and the wide sidewalks give a feeling of spaciousness.

At the corner of Ginza 1-chome, which is straddled by an expressway, there is the Police Museum. You would probably cringe if one of those police motorcycles came chasing after you, but here you can get a photo of yourself riding on one. This is where our tour of Ginza Chuo-dori begins.

When Ginza was first built, apparently there were three concepts: providing a taste of the good side of Western culture and offering the very latest products to shoppers; displaying Japan's modernization to visiting foreigners in the form of a splendid shopping

ピールできる街に、そして火災が再び起こっても、レンガ造りの建物が防火壁の役割を担う防災の街に、というものです。130年余りの時が流れましたが、このコンセプトは今も生きているようです。

　現在、電線や電話線など目障りなものはすべて地下の共同溝に埋設されました。地上には広々とした、見るからに清潔で歩きやすい歩道が両側に伸びています。美しい敷石に注目です。微妙に違う色や模様を見るとそれが天然の御影石だと気づきます。以前この中央通りを走っていた都電の**線路を支えていた敷石**がリサイクルされたものです。そして、そのレール自体も銀座の美しさを可能にした地下の**共同溝**の外枠を支える杭として再利用されています。

　さて銀座1丁目から8丁目まで新橋に向かって歩き始めましょう。ITO-YAという赤いクリップの看板が目に入ります。文房具の銀座・伊東屋です。海外へのお土産にぴったりの和雑貨も豊富にそろっています。4丁目手前、松屋銀座の前に大きな店を構えたアップルストア銀座が目を引きます。人気のマック製品が豊富にそろっています。訪日外国人が家族や友人のために大量に購入する姿が見られます。

　美術館のような落ち着いた店構えを見せるのは御木本真珠店。**養殖した真珠の**

伊東屋
中央区銀座2-7-15
03-3561-8311

松屋銀座
中央区銀座3-6-1
03-3567-1211

Apple
中央区銀座3-5-12
03-5159-8200
無休

district; and building a district that was strong against fires (even if a fire occurred again, the brick buildings would act as a barrier). More than 130 years later, these concepts are still alive today.

Such eyesores as power lines and telephone lines are now all buried in joint conduits running underground. Above ground, clean, broad sidewalks line the thoroughfare on both sides. Note the beautiful paving stones. Looking at the subtly different colors and patterns, you will realize that this is natural granite. The **stones that supported the rails** of the trams that ran along Chuo-dori in the past were recycled and used for the sidewalks. What's more, the rails themselves were recycled as well — as piles to support the outer frames of the underground **joint conduits** that enable Ginza to look so attractive.

Let's start walking from Ginza 1-chome to 8-chome, in the direction of Shinbashi. You will see a sign with a red paperclip that says ITO-YA. This is the Ginza branch of the Ito-ya stationery store. These make ideal gifts and souvenirs. Just before Ginza 4-chome, in front of the Matsuya Ginza, there is the large Apple Store, Ginza. Foreigners visiting Japan can be seen here buying lots of popular Mac products for their family and friends.

The store with the serenity of an art gallery is the pearl shop of the Mikimoto brand, which is famous

ミキモト銀座4丁目本店
中央区銀座4-5-5
03-3535-4611
無休

たった5％弱のみを製品にするというこだわりで世界に知られる日本ブランド、ミキモトです。世界中の女性の首元を真珠で飾りたいという願いから真珠養殖に成功した御木本幸吉の偉業は銀座の一等地に結実しています。ミキモトとミッキーマウス、外国人には似通った発音に聞こえることがあります。世界中の子供たち、そして女性を魅了したのは偶然にも両方ともミッキーなのですね。

木村屋銀座本店
中央区銀座4-5-7
03-3561-0091
無休

その隣には外国人はちょっと苦手なあんことパンを組み合わせた絶妙の**和洋折衷**ヒット商品、銀座のお土産の定番、酒種酵母を使ったあんぱんで知られる木村屋パン店。創業者は、明治維新で仕事にあぶれた木村安兵衛といういわゆる「リストラ武士」でした。安兵衛は、苦心の末に酒種で生地を発酵させたあんぱんを完成させました。その後、明治天皇に気に入られ、**宮内庁御用達**となったことがきっかけで大人気となったのです。

ここを過ぎると日本のタイムズスクエアといわれる銀座4丁目交差点です。この交差点の一角を飾るのが、1932年に服部時計店の本社ビルとして完成し、戦火も免れて今も銀座のシンボルとしてネオ・ルネッサンス様式の外観を誇る高級専門店和光です。和光のウインドーディ

worldwide for its high standards — less than 5 percent of its **cultured pearls** are actually used for making products. Kokichi Mikimoto (1858–1954) dreamed of decorating the necks of women around the world with pearls, and his great achievement in successfully developing the cultured pearl is bearing fruit on this prime site in Ginza. Foreigners often say that "Mikimoto" and "Mickey Mouse" sound the same to them. The character who delights children around the world is "Mickey," and coincidentally, the character who delights women around the world is "Miki," too.

Kimuraya bakery is well known for its bean-jam buns made using sake yeast. Although foreigners tend not to like bean-jam buns very much, they are an excellent **combination of Japanese and Western** tastes and a standard souvenir of Ginza. The founder of the bakery, Yasubei Kimura, was a samurai who became redundant as a result of the Meiji Restoration in 1868. After much hard toil, Yasubei succeeded in developing bean-jam buns by making the dough rise using sake yeast. Emperor Meiji took a liking to them, Kimuraya became a **purveyor to the Imperial Household**, and the buns sold like hotcakes.

Just beyond the Kimuraya bakery is the Ginza 4-chome crossing, which is known as the "Times Square of Japan." At one corner of this intersection stands an imposing building that was constructed in 1932 as the headquarters of the Hattori Tokei-ten watch store. This building survived the war and, with its neo-Renaissance-style exterior, has become a symbol

和光
中央区銀座4-5-11
03-3562-2111
無休

スプレイは1952年から始まりました。幅8メートル、奥行1.5メートル、高さ4メートルの空間には、毎回さまざまな人物や動物など、空想と夢の世界が出現します。銀座を訪れる人々をおもてなしすることをコンセプトに、和光のデザイン・広報部内のデザインチームが担当、企画をしています。ぜひじっくりとご鑑賞ください。そして見上げればもうひとつの銀座のシンボル、時計塔が銀座の町並みを見守り、鐘の音とともに時間を知らせています。

そろそろ朝10時、中央通りのもうひとつの顔、デパートの開店のお時間です。開店時間に間に合うように出かけてみましょう。店長そしてすべての店員の45度の丁寧礼での挨拶を受けながら入店してゆくのはなかなかよい気分です。日本ならではのおもてなしの精神、ここにありです。なんといっても**お客様は神様です**。

デパートで絶対はずせないのは地下の食品売り場です。お目当ては神戸牛。美しい**霜降り**とやわらかさで100グラム3000円です。外国人に「KOBE Beef」として知られていたのは昔のこと。いまや、オーストラリアやアメリカから世界中に輸出されている「WAGYU Beef」が、日本オリジナルの牛肉として世界のグルメのお腹を満たしています。世界中の高

神戸牛：兵庫県で飼育された但馬牛で、指定された規格を満たした牛だけをいう。日本三大和牛のひとつ。

of Ginza. It now houses the exclusive Wako Store. Wako's window displays began in 1952. In a space measuring 8 meters long, 1.5 meters deep, and 4 meters high, a world of fantasy and dreams is created every time featuring various characters, animals, and so on. The design team in Wako's design and public relations department apparently plans and creates these spectacles based on the concept of entertaining visitors to Ginza. It's worth stopping to have a good look at the display. And look upward, too. There you will see another symbol of Ginza, a clock tower that watches over the area and tells the time of the day with a chime.

It will soon be 10 in the morning, which is opening time for Ginza's department stores. Let's make sure we enter at opening time, because then customers are greeted by the store manager and all the staff giving polite, deep bows. For some reason, it makes you feel quite cheery. This is the spirit of hospitality in Japan, where the **customer is almighty**.

If you visit a Japanese department store, there is one place that you really must not miss — the food department in the basement. Look especially for the Kobe beef. Japanese beef, which is famous for its **marbled texture** and tenderness, costs about ¥3,000 per 100 grams. In the past, the beef was called "KOBE Beef" by foreigners. Now, exported from Australia and the U.S., "WAGYU Beef" is the original Japanese beef that satisfies the stomachs of gourmets around

級レストランで人気が出始めており、もはや、日本の**専売特許**ではないのです。しかし、ここでひるんでいるわけにはいきません。日本で生まれ育った、優良で純粋遺伝子を持つ「WAGYU」ではなく漢字の「和牛」がケースに並んでいるところを見ていただきましょう。**量ではなく質で勝負**のmade in Japanビーフです。

　そのおいしさの秘密が特別な飼育法にあるのはよく知られています。牛は食欲増進のためにビールを振る舞われ、ご機嫌になり、クラシック音楽の流れる牛舎でマッサージまで受けています。値段にビール代やマッサージ代が入っているのは当然。ところで和牛はひとこと英語をしゃべるのをご存知でしょうか？ もっとビール！ もっとマッサージ！ つまり、「more, more…」とおねだりをするのだそうです。

　日本で一番高い価格の土地が存在するのも決まって銀座です。数年前までは4丁目交差点の交番がある角から2軒目の濃いあずき色の建物、**書画用品・香の老舗専門店鳩居堂**の前の土地価格が日本最高でした。一歩、進むごとに2〜300万円です。土地価格は税金に反映されるので、銀座の地主は、莫大な税金を払わなくてはなりません。**想像を超えた金額**です。商品価格が幾分高額なのも納得です。1杯800円のコーヒーを高いと思うか否

鳩居堂
中央区銀座5-7-4
03-3571-4429

歴史は古く熊谷直実（鎌倉初期の武士）まで遡る。江戸時代に入り、京都で薬商を初め、その後中国から筆墨を輸入し文具を扱いはじめ、現在に至る。

the world. Wagyu is beginning to gain popularity in high-end restaurants around the world. It is no longer **exclusive** to Japan. But do not be deceived. Take a look at the beef arranged in the display case. It has the Chinese character 和牛 (wagyu), rather than the English word "Wagyu," meaning that this beef has been raised in Japan and has excellent and pure genetics. This is made in Japan beef where it is **quality rather than quantity that counts**.

The secret of the delicious meat, as is well known, lies in the special breeding method. The cows are treated to beer in order to boost their appetites and put them in a good mood, and they are given massages as classical music plays in their cow sheds. Naturally, the price includes the cost of the beer and massages. By the way, did you know that Japanese cows know a bit of English? When they want more beer or massage, they moo "more, more."

Ginza, inevitably, also has the most valuable area of land in Japan. Until a few years ago, the most expensive plot of land in Japan was in front of Kyukyodo, a long-established specialty store for **calligraphy, painting supplies and incense**. It is a dark reddish-brown building, the second from the corner of Ginza 4-chome crossing and its police box. One step was the equivalent of ¥2 million to ¥3 million! Since land prices are reflected in taxes, Ginza landowners have to pay enormous taxes — **quite unimaginable sums**. So you can understand why

か？　単なる1杯のコーヒーへの対価ではなく、日本一高価な土地、銀座で飲むという**付加価値**つきのコーヒーの値段ですと説明しますが、外国人にはどうも**腑に落ちない**ようすです。

　そのまま晴海通りを進み数寄屋橋交差点角の交番の後ろの西銀座（NISHIGINZA）の1、2階には今や世界ブランド・ハローキティグッズの日本**随一**・最大店があります。エスカレーターを上ると世界は一瞬にしてサンリオワールド、フロアーには数百、数千のキティちゃんが溢れ、女の子も淑女も幸せな歓声を上げます。

　さて、紳士のあなたにはジャパニーズクール、サムライの刀をじっくりとご覧いただけるスポットをご紹介します。西洋の剣は突く、日本の刀は斬りおろすもの。そのために切先に向かって銀色に輝くそりが特徴の美術品、日本刀が生まれました。晴海通りを渡って反対側の高速道路の下の銀座ファイブの2階にある日本刀専門店「誠友堂」には大小の刀剣、つば、目貫、甲冑などが展示販売されています。傷がついてしまった小刀を手に“かわいそうに……”と語る代表取締役・生野正氏の鑑識眼で選ばれた品々をご覧

西銀座
（NISHIGINZA）
中央区銀座4-1
03-3566-4111

Sanrio World
GINZA
西銀座（NISHIGINZA）
1・2階
03-3566-4040

銀座ファイブ
中央区銀座5-1
03-3571-0487

誠友堂
銀座ファイブ2階
03-3558-8001

the prices of goods in Ginza are a little exorbitant. Is an ¥800 cup of coffee expensive? They say that you are paying not simply for a cup of coffee but also for the **added value** of drinking it in Ginza, the most expensive place in Japan. But that explanation does **not** seem to **go down** with foreigners.

If you go further along Harumi-dori until you reach the Sukiyabashi Bridge intersection, you will find the NISHIGINZA behind the police box on the corner. On the first and the second floor is, **without rival**, the largest Japanese store dealing in products associated with the now worldwide Hello Kitty brand. Going up the escalator, you enter a seemingly different realm of being. This is the Sanrio World floor, overflowing with hundreds, no thousands, of Kitties, bringing screams of delight from the youngest girls and the most elegant ladies alike.

For men, there is a spot where you can treat your eyes to one of the finest aspects of cool Japan, the samurai sword. The Western sword is made for thrusting, the Japanese sword for striking. That is why the Japanese sword, a **work of art** in itself, has a gleaming silver curve reaching out to its tip. Crossing over to the opposite side of Harumi-dori, under the expressway, we go up to the second floor of GINZA 5 FIVE, where you find Seiyudo, a shop that specializes in Japanese swords, displaying and selling large and small swords, guards, the ornaments on the guards called *menuki*, armor, and still more. You can enjoy the many objects selected by the expert eye of the

ください。端正な細工を施された目貫は女性にも人気です。海外には2週間ほどの手続きを経て配送手配もしてくれます。

他にも骨董品専門店が数店舗並んでいます。きもの地をドレスやコートなどに仕立て直す専門店「百人一趣」では和と洋のファッションのいいとこどりが手に入ります。このドレスでパーティーでは話題の中心になれそうです。

もう一度中央通りへ戻り、7丁目の資生堂パーラーのご紹介です。資生堂はもとは日本初の西洋医学による**調剤薬局店**でした。創業者がアメリカ訪問時に見たドラッグストアを参考にして、食品や雑貨、そして化粧品も扱うことになりました。レストラン経営も長い歴史があります。1928年開業、メイド・イン・ジャパンの西洋料理店第1号です。伝統的メニューのミートクロケットとアイスクリームで銀座のランチは完成です。少々お値段が張りますが、窓から中央通りの風景を見下ろしながらゆったりと味わってみてください。**ここでひとこと**、昔は銀貨が作られていたのに、今はお金が費やされる街、それが銀座です。

百人一趣
中央区銀座5-1 銀座
ファイブ2階 ジェットジュエリー・ラハ内
03-3571-0035

資生堂パーラー
中央区銀座8-8-3
4・5階
03-5537-6241
月曜定休

managing director, Tadashi Ikuno, who you might see with a damaged short sword in his hand, saying, "The poor thing..." The small, delicately sculptured *menuki* are also a favorite among the ladies. Given a couple weeks for the paperwork, the shop will ship your purchases overseas.

On this floor there are a number of other antique shops. One shop, Hyakunin Isshu, will make you a dress or coat using kimono cloth, combining the best of Eastern and Western fashion. Wearing such a dress to a party would surely make you the center of attention.

Let's go back to Chuo-dori and visit the Shiseido Parlor at Ginza 7-chome. Originally Shiseido was Japan's first **dispensing pharmacy** for Western medicine. The founder got the hint to handle food products, sundry goods, and cosmetics as well after seeing drugstores during a visit to the United States. Shiseido's restaurant business has a long history, too. Opened in 1928, it was the first "made in Japan" Western restaurant. A meat croquette and ice cream from the traditional menu completes your lunch in Ginza. It might be a little expensive, but you can relax here and enjoy the view of Ginza through the window. And while you are gazing, **here is a little thought for the day**: In the past Ginza was a place where money was minted; today Ginza is a place where money is spent.

いよ！ 待ってました〜！ の
歌舞伎座から築地・浜離宮へ
"That's What I've Been Waiting For!": Kabukiza, Tsukiji, and Hamarikyu

for Roppongi & Nakamegur
六本木・中目黒方面

Chuo-do
中央通

Ginza Line
銀座線

Metropolitan Expressway
首都高速道路

for Akasakamitsuke & Shibuya
赤坂見附・渋谷方面

Shinbashi Station
新橋駅

Toei Asakusa Line
都営浅草線

for Gotanda & Asakusa
五反田・浅草方面

Shiodome
汐留

N

Hama Detached Palace Gard
浜離宮

for Rainbow Bridge
レインボーブリッジ

for Ueno & Asakusa
上野・浅草方面

Ginza Station
銀座駅

Hibiya Line
日比谷線

for Asakusa
浅草方面

Higashi-Ginza Station
東銀座駅

Kabukiza
歌舞伎座

Harumi-dori
晴海通り

Showa-dori
昭和通り

Metropolitan Expressway
首都高速道路

for Ueno & Oshiage
上野・押上方面

Tsukiji Station
築地駅

for Roppongi & Shinjuku
六本木・新宿方面

Tsukiji Honganji Temple
築地本願寺

Tsukijishijo Station
築地市場駅

Tsukiji Outside Market
築地場外市場

Kachidokibashi Bridge
勝鬨橋

Toei Oedo Line
大江戸線

Sumida River
隅田川

Tsukiji River
築地川

Tsukiji Market
築地市場

for Ueno-okachimachi & Iidabashi
上野御徒町・飯田橋方面

歌舞伎座

歌舞伎座
中央区銀座4-12-15
03-3545-6800

　1889年、日本一の大劇場と銘打って開場した歌舞伎座は漏電による焼失再建後、関東大震災、空襲を乗り越えて2013年5回目の**改築**が完成し、バリアフリー、トイレの充実、アクセスの良さに加えて、趣向をこらしたおもてなしのサービスで迎えてくれます。

　地下鉄日比谷線の東銀座駅から直結している木挽町広場は完全に歌舞伎空間です。歌舞伎座の地下2階にあって**だれでも入れます**。歌舞伎グッズの買い物はもちろん、歌舞伎写真館で役者になりきって記念写真はいかがでしょうか。伝統の歌舞伎メーク、衣装や背景など本物に囲まれ役者気分で、はい！ ポーズ。またとないお土産です。

　観劇には、G-marc Guide「字幕ガイド」がおすすめアイテムです。玄関入り口の階段を上り、右へ進むと受付カウンターがあります。有料（1台1000円）ですが、英語あるいは日本語による解説が舞台の進行と同時に随時流れてくる優れものです。筋書きや役者の動きの意味、見所が

Kabukiza

Dedicated to the traditional drama of Kabuki, the Kabukiza first opened in 1889 as the largest theater in Japan, but it was subsequently burned down due to an electrical shortage. The theater was rebuilt, only to be destroyed again in the Great Kanto Earthquake in 1923, then reconstructed and destroyed once more in the bombing of Tokyo during World War II. In 2013 its **fifth rebuilding** was completed with the comfort of theatergoers fully in mind, including a barrier-free environment, enhanced toilet facilities, and improved accessibility.

The Higashi Ginza Station on the Metro Hibiya Line is directly connected to the Kobikicho Plaza, which is an integral part of the Kabuki world. It is located in the level 2 basement of the theater and is **fully open to the public**. There you can shop for Kabuki-related goods or have your picture taken in the guise of a Kabuki actor, including costumes, makeup, background, and everything else. Just say "Cheese" and you have the perfect souvenir.

When watching Kabuki, the G-marc Guide (captioning) service is recommended. Go up the stairs at the entrance and turn right to find the reception counter. There is a fee (1,000 yen per unit), but it is an excellent device that provides commentary in English or Japanese as the play progresses. The guide also gives a detailed explanation of the storyline, the

懇切丁寧に説明されるので、歌舞伎初心者や外国人、そして歌舞伎マニアの方にも人気があります。

歌舞伎は今では男役者だけで演じられていますが、そもそもは現在の島根県、出雲から京都にやってきた女芸人の阿国が、鴨川の河原でそれまでなかった斬新な踊りを披露し、都人を魅了したのがその起源とされています。その異様な姿と**煽動的な踊り**は人々を惑わすとされ、まもなく禁止されてしまいます。京都の四条大橋のたもとに出雲阿国の銅像がありますが、男装で刀を差し、扇を持ってポーズをとっている姿は優雅でなぜ禁止されたのか戸惑うほどです。

出雲阿国：出身は出雲大社の巫女とも言われるが定かではない。彼女の念仏踊りが、後に歌舞伎に発展。

京都から江戸へと歌舞伎は広まり、男歌舞伎へと変わってゆきます。歌舞伎は、芝居と踊りと音楽が融合した日本の伝統舞台芸能です。外国人には「日本のオペラ」と紹介しています。女形の存在、花道での客席と役者の接近した緊張感、回り舞台やせり上がりのからくり、ひな壇に並ぶ三味線や笛、太鼓の囃子連中と長唄、役者の美しい衣裳、強調されたメークアップなど、楽しみは山とあります。

新しくなった歌舞伎座タワー

meaning of the actors' movements, and the highlights, so it is popular with not only novices and foreigners but also Kabuki enthusiasts.

Although Kabuki is performed now by male actors only, its origins are said to lie in a sensational new dance performed in 1603 on the dry bed of the Kamogawa River in Kyoto by a women's theatrical troupe led by Okuni, who had been a female attendant at the Izumo Shrine in what is now Shimane Prefecture. The **provocative dance** apparently excited the townspeople of Kyoto so much that it was soon prohibited. There is a bronze statue of Okuni at the foot of the Shijo-Ohashi Bridge in Kyoto. Looking at this statue, in which she strikes an elegant pose, dressed as a man, wielding a sword, and holding a fan, it is hard to understand why she was banned.

Kabuki subsequently spread from Kyoto to Edo and transformed into a style of theater performed by men. Today it is one of Japan's traditional performing arts, combining drama, dancing, and music. Kabuki is often introduced to foreigners as "Japanese opera." **There are lots of things that will catch your eye**, such as the *onnagata* (female impersonators); the heightened tension when an actor appears on the *hanamichi* (elevated runway extending into the auditorium), bringing him closer to the audience; the revolving stage and trapdoor mechanism; the musicians seated on a tiered platform, with their *shamisen* (three-stringed plucked lutes), flutes, and drums, and the *nagauta* songs; the beautiful costumes

観客席全体は、左右に桟敷席、舞台に向かって左には花道、天井は4階まで吹き抜けの心まで晴れやかになりそうな広々した空間です。舞台の幕が上がったら、あとはG-marc Guideを読みながら400年の伝統舞台芸術を堪能してください。**限られた時間しかない方には一幕見**をおすすめします。チケット売り場は玄関向かって左側にあり、エレベーターで4階に上ります。舞台ははるかかなたで、役者が出入りする大切な舞台の一部の花道も、その足音が聞こえるだけで見えません。

しかし、舞台だけでなくおまけの楽しみがあります。「おとわや〜！」「なりこまや〜！」「いよ！ 待ってました〜！」などとタイミングよく役者へ声をかける大向こうさんが、毎日交代で陣取るところなのです。大向こうグループと呼ばれる会が3つあり、毎日必ず一人はこの重要な仕事のためにボランティアで駆けつけます。声かけがない芝居は**まるで塩がふってない焼き魚**です。**味気ないことこのうえなし**です。突然、隣の人が大声で叫ぶのですから、知らないで座っていた外国人は本当にびっくりします。事前にこれらのチアリーダーのことを教えてあげておいてください。

大向こうグループ：東京には、弥生会、寿会、声友会の3つがある。

of the actors; and their accentuated makeup.

The auditorium itself is spacious, rising airily up to the fourth floor. There are box seats to the left and right. The hanamichi is to the left as you face the stage. Once the curtain rises, you can read the G-marc Guide and enjoy this 400-year-old traditional performing art. **For those of you with limited time**, I recommend watching only one scene. Tickets are sold at the ticket counter on the left side of the entrance as you go in, and you can proceed to the fourth floor by elevator. The stage is somewhat in the distance, and the all-important *hanamichi*, by which actors make entrances and exits to the stage, cannot be seen; only the footfalls of the actors can be heard.

Yet, in addition to the stage, there is an extra bonus. Don't be startled when you hear members of the audience calling out, at appropriate times, the house names of actors, such as "Otowaya!" and "Narikomaya!" and things like "That's just what I've been waiting for!" These people are called, like their seats, *omuko*, and they are die-hard Kabuki fans. There are three groups of omuko, and every day they will dispatch at least one volunteer to do this important job. They say that a play without such yelling from the audience is **like a grilled fish without salt**. **There is nothing more flavorless.** Foreigners who are not aware of this custom tend to be astonished when a member of the audience suddenly shouts out in this manner, so if you have the chance, let them know beforehand about these "cheerleaders."

歌舞伎を楽しむのはいまだに女性が大半を占めています。舞台の上の役者よろしく、着物姿も美しい桟敷席で観劇をしている奥方やお嬢様を目にすると、華やかさで楽しさも倍増です。**江戸っ子の楽しみといえば**、男性は相撲と吉原、女性は歌舞伎と**相場が決まっていた**ようです。今では明るすぎるほどの照明で浮かび上がる舞台ですが、江戸時代はろうそくと外からの太陽光だけで役者の顔や舞台装置を見ていたのです。当然舞台は午前中から日が暮れるまで。大店の奥方やお嬢様たちは前の晩から劇場近くに宿泊し、朝から身支度をしていそいそと出かけていったとか。**1泊2日の観劇**はさぞかし楽しい小旅行のようなものだったことでしょう。

築地場外市場

　将軍の**御膝元**、日本橋にあった**魚河岸**は1923年の関東大震災で壊滅。その後、築地に移転し、世界一の漁獲取扱量を誇った築地ブランドが生まれました。しかし、設備の老朽化のため、2016年に場外市場のみを残してすべてが豊洲に移転しました。午前3時に列に並んで見学したまぐろのセリ場や、高級すし店や老舗

The majority of people who go to watch Kabuki are still women. As well as the actors on the stage, the sight of the kimono-clad ladies and their daughters watching from the box seats adds to the enjoyment. The pastimes of **Edoites** seem to **have been pretty much standard**: sumo wrestling and the Yoshiwara bordellos for men and Kabuki for women. Although the Kabuki stage now is illuminated by lighting that sometimes even seems to be too strong, in the Edo Period the audience watched the actors' faces and the props with only the help of candles and outside light. Naturally, therefore, performances were held from the morning until sundown. You can just imagine the wife of some large shop owner and her daughters staying at a lodging place near the theater the night before and then in the morning dressing up and setting off cheerfully for the performance. No doubt the **overnight trip and theater visit** was a pleasant little outing for them.

Tsukiji Outer Market

The **fish market** in Nihonbashi, the **heart** of the shogun's domain, was destroyed in the Great Kanto Earthquake of 1923. It was later relocated to Tsukiji, where Tsukiji's reputation was born, boasting the largest volume of fish products handled anywhere in the world. However, due to aging facilities, the entire market was moved to Toyosu in 2016, leaving only the exterior fish market. The tuna auction house, which

料亭の**板前**が自らおとずれて、値踏みをし、買い付けをしていた仲卸売場も、すべてが、近未来的な豊洲の建物に収まり、見学コースからガラス越しに見下ろす形になりました。

　さて、それでは築地の現在はどうなったのか。市場の跡地には再開発計画が決まり、**MICE施設**が軸になります。そして場外市場は多くの観光客を惹きつける観光スポットとして健在です。

　築地は江戸時代に埋め立てられました。埋め立て工事は海から寄せてくる波との格闘が避けられません。その波をよけてくれる神様を祀っているのが、波除(なみよけ)神社です。場外市場の見学はこの神社から始めましょう。この地で商売を長年してきた人々を精神的に支えてきました。まずは鳥居をくぐると、左右にある大きな獅子頭が目を引きます。右側は黒いお顔に金色の大きな口の雄獅子、左側は真っ赤な顔に金色のひげとお歯黒が愛嬌な雌獅子の頭です。それぞれ1トンもあり、年に一度6月に開催される**築地獅子祭**で、この対の獅子頭はこの界隈に引き出されます。雌獅子は女性のみで担がれるのが珍しい光景になります。

　さて、この雌獅子が祀ってあるお堂のとなりに、東京鶏卵加工業組合が建立し

波除神社
中央区築地6-20-37
03-3541-8451

visitors had to line up for at 3 a.m., and the wholesale market, where **chefs** from high-class sushi restaurants and long-established Japanese restaurants used to come to check the prices and make their purchases are now all housed in a futuristic building in Toyosu, where there is a self-guided tour during which visitors can look down on everything from behind glass.

So, what has become of Tsukiji now? A redevelopment plan has been decided on for the former market site, with a **MICE (meetings, incentives, conferences, and exhibitions) facility** at its core. And the market is still going strong as a tourist spot.

Tsukiji was reclaimed in the Edo Period. The reclamation work was a battle with waves coming in from the sea, so Namiyoke Inari Shrine was built to worship the god that keeps the waves away. Let's start our tour of the market from this shrine. This structure enshrines the gods who have provided spiritual support to the people who have done business here for many years. As you pass through the *torii* gate, you will notice large lion heads on either side of the gate. On the right is a male lion with a black face and a large golden mouth, and on the left is a female lion with a bright red face, golden beard, and black teeth. Each lion head weighs one ton, and the pair is brought out to the area once a year in June for the **Tsukiji Lion Festival**. The female lioness is carried only by women, which is rare for a Japanese festival.

Next to the hall where the female lioness is enshrined, there is an egg monument built by the

た玉子塚、次に、寿司塚、海老塚、ハマ
グリ石、鮟鱇塚が並んでいます。それぞ
れの命をいただき、商売をしてきた人々
が感謝して祀っているのですが、**なんで
も祀ってしまう日本の不思議**を真面目に
語ってみてください。美味しい食事は人
を幸せにします。日本では、幸せにして
くれるものこそ、神様なのです。

　それではお祈りの場を出て、場外市場
をご案内しましょう。人の口に入る食べ
物ならなんでもあり、お腹がすいたら天
下一品の海鮮丼で即解決。そしてまた買
い物めぐりを楽しんでください。

　2013年、ユネスコは和食を無形文化遺
産に登録しました。「多様で新鮮な食材」
「バランスのよい健康的な食事」「四季そ
れぞれを表現し、多彩に巡ってくる年中
行事の折に特別にその時だけ料理される
伝統の料理」が選ばれた理由です。**和食
の料理法は5つあります**。1番目は炊く、
2番目は焼く、3番目は茹でる、4番目は
揚げる、そして残る5番目は、熱を加え
て料理をしない、つまり生のままです。
　一番難しいのはなんといっても5番目
でしょう。生のままといっても、プロの
技がさえるのが魚の切り身を和包丁でい
かにその細胞を傷付けずに表面を滑らか
に切り分けるかです。ガイドを分かりや

Tokyo Chicken and Egg Processing Association, followed by a sushi monument, a shrimp monument, a clam monument, and a monkfish monument. Each of these is enshrined by the people who work in the business in gratitude for the lives they have given up. Please be serious when you describe the **wonders of a country like Japan where everything is enshrined**. Good meals bring people happiness. In Japan, our gods are the things that make us happy.

Now let's leave the prayer hall and take a tour of the market outside. If it is a food that people can put in their mouths, you can find it here, and if you get hungry, a bowl of Kaisen-don (seafood on rice) at Tenka Ippin will solve the problem immediately. Then, how about another shopping spree?

In 2013, UNESCO registered Japanese food as an Intangible Cultural Heritage. The reasons why Japanese food was chosen were "diverse and fresh ingredients," "a balanced and healthy diet," and "traditional dishes that express each of the four seasons and are specially prepared for various annual events." **There are five ways to cook Japanese food**: the first is simmering, the second is baking, the third is boiling, the fourth is frying, and lastly, the fifth is not cooking with heat, i.e. serving it raw.

The fifth is probably the most difficult. Although it is just raw food, the most difficult part is to cut the fish fillet with a knife without damaging its cells. One way to make a guide's explanation easier to understand is to **talk specifically about the differences** between

すくする手法のひとつは、相手の国と**日本の違いを具体的に話す**ことです。和包丁と洋包丁の違いの説明は、さばく食材の違いから始めます。肉なのか魚なのか？　硬いのか柔らかいのか？　**押し切りなのか、引き切りなのか**です。和包丁は柔らかな魚を引き切るために、切れ味が鋭く魚の表面を傷付けない片刃です。肉を押し切るのは両刃の洋包丁です。刃先の断面は洋包丁はアルファベットのV、和包丁はカタカナのレの形をしています。片刃の方が鋭利です。

　市場には包丁専門店が何軒もあります。美味しいものを目当てにぶらぶら歩くも良し、しかし、調理する目で見るのも一興です。新鮮な魚の切り身や刺身を見て、料理好きな方とわかったら包丁専門店に立ち寄って、さまざまな長さや、食材や料理法別にそのデザインや形も違う包丁が種類豊富に陳列された店内を見るのもおすすめです。魚を捌く出刃庖丁、刺身包丁、皿の模様が見えるほどに薄くフグを切り分けるためのフグ包丁、野菜を切る菜切包丁、カリフォルニアロールを切る寿司切包丁など、目的に応じて選べます。おすすめのタイプはお店の人に相談して決めてください。

Japan and the other person's country. To explain the difference between Japanese and Western kitchen knives, start with the difference in the ingredients to be cut. Is it meat or fish? Is it hard or soft? **Is it a push cut or a pull cut?** Japanese kitchen knives have a single blade to cut soft fish without damaging the surface of the fish. A double-edged Western kitchen knife is used to push through meat. The cross-section of the cutting edge is the shape of the letter "V" for Western kitchen knives and the shape of the Japanese character "レ" for Japanese kitchen knives. Single-edged knives are sharper.

There are several stores specializing in kitchen knives in the market. Wandering around the market for delicious food is good, but looking at it with the eyes of a chef is **also a treat**. Look at the fresh fish fillets and sashimi, and if you like to cook, stop by a knife store and see the wide variety of knives of different lengths, designs, and shapes for different ingredients and cooking methods. You can choose a knife according to your purpose, such as a *deba bocho* knife for cutting fish, a sashimi knife, a puffer fish knife to cut so thinly that you can see the pattern on the plate, a vegetable knife, and a sushi knife to cut California rolls. Consult a shopkeeper to decide which type is best for you.

浜離宮恩賜庭園
中央区浜離宮園1-1
03-3541-0200

浜離宮

　築地場外市場から数分ほど足を伸ばして、将軍のお庭として都内で一番格の高い浜離宮を楽しんでみましょう。浅草・吾妻橋から水上バスで隅田川をくだりこの御庭を訪れるツアーも人気です。1654年に時の4代将軍の弟・松平綱重が**別邸**を建てたのが始まりで、その後、幾度かの改修を経て、11代の徳川家斉のころに現在の姿になりました。将軍お気に入りの鴨猟の場、薬草や塩、砂糖の製造をした実験作業農園、はるばるベトナムを経て来訪した象の飼育場、江戸城を守る**出城**、将軍が乗る舟の上がり場。明治の時代になり、皇室の離宮となったのち、外国からの賓客をもてなす迎賓館が建設されたおもてなしの場、など、将軍から天皇へ、そして、都民の庭園として、持ち主が代わっても、常に東京を代表する庭園として堂々と存続してきました。

　入園チケット売り場で全体地図を手に入れてお目当ての場所を確認。まずは、二つ残っている鴨場のうち、中央の池の近くにある庚申堂鴨場に向かいます。芝生に覆われた人間の背の高さ程度の小山

Hama Detached Palace Garden (Hamarikyu Teien)

A few minutes' walk from the Tsukiji Outdoor Market, you can enjoy Hama Rikyu. Belonging to the shogun, it was the most prestigious of Tokyo's gardens. Tours by waterbus down the Sumida-gawa River from Asakusa or Azuma-bashi are also popular. In 1654, Matsudaira Tsunashige, the younger brother of the fourth shogun, built a **villa** here, and after several renovations, it took on its present form during the reign of the 11th Tokugawa shogun, Ienari. It was the Shogun's favorite place for duck hunting, an experimental farm for the production of medicinal herbs, salt, and sugar, a breeding ground for an elephant that came all the way from Vietnam, a **fort** for the protection of Edo Castle, and a landing for the Shogun's boats. It also became a place for hospitality when a guesthouse was built to receive guests from abroad after it became an imperial residence in the Meiji Period. From the shogun to the emperor, and then for the people of Tokyo, Hama Rikyu has always remained one of the most well-known gardens in Tokyo, even though its owners have changed.

Get a map of the whole area at the ticket office and check the locations you wish to visit. First, head to Koshindo Kamoba, one of the two remaining duck ponds, located near the central pond. It is a small, grass-covered hill about the height of a person with a

で、**台形**に中央が切り取られ木枠で囲まれ、小さなのぞき窓と餌を投入する筒、そして、木版が横に下がっています。ここで、想像もつかない、珍しい鴨猟の方法を紹介しましょう。

のぞき窓から見ると、長い引堀がまっすぐ伸び、その先に大きな池の一部が見えます。池は元溜まりと呼ばれ、そこには囮の飛べない鴨が飼われています。餌付けは板を叩くことで知らされます。引堀に入ってくる囮鴨を追ってついてきた野生の鴨を、覗き窓から見届けて、頃合いを見て、引堀近くで**鷹匠**が鷹を飛ばして鴨を捕らえるのです。明治時代になってからは鷹ではなく、網で捕えました。11代将軍家斉は大の**鷹狩**好きで、合計で170回近く楽しんだという記録があります。その際休憩所として使ったといわれる茶屋3棟が、2010年から2018年にわたって中央池近くに再建されました。それぞれ、松の茶屋、燕の茶屋、そして、一番重要とされた鷹の茶屋です。鷹の茶屋は下足のまま休めるデザインで屋久杉やヒノキなど最高の木材をふんだんに使い、建設費用は2.3億円でした。

池の中心にある中島のお茶屋にはヒノキのお伝え橋を渡ってゆきます。和室でお茶を楽しんだり、周りにめぐらせた縁側では東京湾から渡ってくる海風をかす

trapezoid shape cut out in the center and surrounded by a wooden frame with a small peephole, a tube for feeding, and a wooden plate hanging down beside it. You would never imagine the unusual method of duck hunting that I am going to describe here.

Looking through the peephole, you can see a long moat stretching straight out and part of a large pond at the end of it. The pond is called Motodamari, and it is where they keep flightless ducks that act as **decoys**. The ducks were notified that it was feeding time by hitting a board. The wild ducks that follow the decoys into the moat were watched through a peephole, and when the time was right, a **falconer** would fly a hawk near the moat to catch the ducks. In the Meiji Period, ducks were caught not with hawks but with nets. The 11th shogun, Ienari, was a big fan of **falconry**, and records indicate that he engaged in it nearly 170 times in total. Three teahouses, which are said to have been used as resting places during falconry events, were rebuilt near the central pond between 2010 to 2018. They are the Pine Teahouse, the Swallow Teahouse, and the Hawk Teahouse, which was considered the most important. The Hawk's Teahouse was designed to allow people to rest without removing their shoes and was built with the finest woods, such as cypress and Yakushima cedar, at a cost of 2.3 million yen.

The teahouse is located in the center of the pond and is accessed via a cypress bridge. Enjoy a cup of tea in the Japanese-style room, and feel the sea breeze coming from Tokyo Bay on the surrounding veranda.

かに感じてみましょう。浜離宮の一番の特徴はその水源。隅田川と東京湾からの海水が混ざった汽水の出入りが、5つの水門によって調整され、潮の干満によって景観が変化します。将軍達のお気に入りの庭だったのは当然です。

　もう一つの話題を紹介します。明治時代になって皇室の離宮に変わった浜離宮に、外国からの賓客をもてなす迎賓館（延遼館）が建設されました。現在は大手門の南側の芝生公園となっている場所にあり、アメリカ合衆国から来日した元18代大統領グラント氏も2カ月間その迎賓館に滞在しました。滞在中、中の茶屋で明治天皇と2時間近く、当時の列強国のアジアへの野心や、公選議会や琉球問題、条約改正、教育などの問題について話しあったという記録が残っています。明治維新から11年後、まだ日本は世界の動きについては限られた知識しかなかった時代に、当時、若き27歳だった明治天皇がどう受け止めたのか。その後、日本の進んだ道を決めるきっかけとなる瞬間の舞台だったかもしれません。

The most distinctive feature of Hama Rikyu is its water source. It is **brackish water** that is a mixture of water from the ocean and the Sumida-gawa River. There are five **sluice gates** to adjust the water, and the scenery changes with the ebb and flow of the tide. It is no wonder the garden was a favorite of the shoguns.

There is one more thing I would like to tell you about. In the Meiji Period, a guesthouse to entertain visitors from abroad (the Enryokan) was constructed in Hama Rikyu, which had been converted into an imperial villa. It was located near the lawn on the south side of the present Otemon Gate. The former 18th President of the United States, Ulysses S. Grant, stayed there for two months. Records indicate that during his stay there, Grant spent nearly two hours in the teahouse discussing the ambitions of the powerful nations of the time toward Asia, the **public elected assembly**, the Ryukyu Islands issue, **treaty revisions**, education, and other issues with the emperor. Eleven years after the Meiji Restoration, at a time when Japan still had limited knowledge of the world's movements, it may have been the setting for the moment when the young, 27-year-old Emperor Meiji accepted the advice and determined the path Japan took thereafter.

明治の杜と原宿
Meiji Forest and Shrine:
Harajuku

← **for Shibuya & Shinagawa**
渋谷・品川方面

JR Yamanote Line
山手線

Meijijingumae Station
明治神宮前駅

↖ **for Shibuya**
渋谷方面

Meiji-dori
明治通り

Ota Museu
太田記念美術

Meijijingumae Station
明治神宮前駅

Kamawa
かまわ

Omotesando-dori
表参道

Chiyoda Line
千代田線

← **for Shibuya**
渋谷方面

Hanzomon Line
半蔵門線

Omotesando Station
表参道駅

for Ayase
綾瀬方面

for Akasakamitsuke
赤坂見附方面

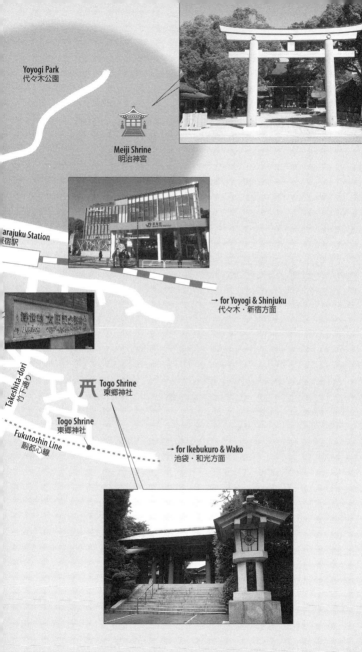

Yoyogi Park
代々木公園

Meiji Shrine
明治神宮

arajuku Station
宿駅

→ for Yoyogi & Shinjuku
代々木・新宿方面

Takeshita-dori
竹下通り

Togo Shrine
東郷神社

Togo Shrine
東郷神社

Fukutoshin Line
副都心線

→ for Ikebukuro & Wako
池袋・和光方面

明治神宮

　武家社会が終焉を迎え、近代日本が生まれたとき、江戸城から西の一帯にあった名だたる譜代大名の豪奢な屋敷は取り壊され、代わりに新生日本を象徴する建物や施設が**続々と**建設されました。ここでは近代化の大きな流れの中、重要な役割を果たした二人の人物ゆかりの地を訪ねながら、江戸、明治、そして現代と、目覚ましい発展をとげた表参道周辺をご案内します。

明治天皇：在位1867–1912。1867年に王政復古の大号令を発し、翌年、元号を明治と改める。江戸を東京と改め、新政府のもと日本の近代化を進めた。

　まずは明治天皇です。日本が開国後、西洋列国に伍して近代国家を建設してゆく中、欧米に範をとって**立憲君主制**をしいた新生日本の中心にいたのが明治天皇です。45年の間在位し、その60年の生涯を閉じたとき、この天皇を祭る神社建設運動が起こりました。多くの候補地の中から選ばれた代々木の地には、神社にあるべき**鎮守の森**がありませんでした。永遠の森をどうやって創り出すのか、明治の人々の英知が試されることになったのです。

　原宿駅を降りてすぐ、JRの線路をまたぐ橋を渡るとそこは都会のオアシス。17

Meiji Shrine

At the time when **feudal society** was coming to an end and modern Japan was being born, the luxurious residences of the daimyo lords that had occupied the area to the west of Edo Castle were pulled down, and in their place many buildings and facilities symbolizing the new Japan were constructed **in rapid succession**. Let us take a look around the Omotesando district, which achieved spectacular development in the transition from the Edo to the Meiji Period and into modern times, in particular visiting places connected with two figures who played important roles amid the general trend of modernization.

The first of these historical figures was Emperor Meiji. As Japan, after its opening, set about building a modern state on a par with Western countries, it was Emperor Meiji who was at the center of the newborn state that adopted a system of **constitutional monarchy** modeled after the West. Emperor Meiji reigned for 45 years. When he died at the age of 60, a movement began to construct a shrine dedicated to his soul. The district of Yoyogi in Tokyo was chosen from among many candidate sites, but it did not have any **woodland**, which was essential for a shrine. The people of that time racked their brains over the question of how to create an eternal forest.

Exiting Harajuku Station and crossing the nearby bridge over the JR railway lines, you come to a real

明治神宮
渋谷区代々木神園町
1-1
03-3379-5511

1920年創建された
が、1945年の大空襲
で創建当初の建物の
ほとんどが消失。そ
の後、1958年に復興
造営が完成。

万本の木々に守られた明治神宮です。水
の流れにもまれて玉のように磨かれた清
浄な小石を境内や参道に敷き詰めるの
は神社のルール。威厳あふれる一の鳥居
から玉砂利を踏む音を確かめながら大鳥
居まで来ると、すぐその右手の森の中に
堂々と成長した大木が数本、大きな枝を
伸ばしています。

鳥居のすぐ右側からクスノキ、スダジ
イ、アラカシ、シラカシ、アカガシと並
んでいます。自然界ではもともとあり得
ない木々の配列です。理由はもちろん、
当時植林された木々がみごとに鎮守の森
に成長したからです。今からほぼ100年
前、10万本におよぶ全国からの献木を7
年かけて植林してできたものなのです。
今では植林した人々の気配が感じられな
いほど自然を感じる森ですが、明治の
人々の英知とたゆまぬ努力の結晶なので
す。

キリスト教の大聖堂の祭壇には十字架
のキリスト像、天井には光り輝く神の国
が象徴的にデザインされています。神は
天上高くおわしますと、人々は高き処へ
祈りを奉げます。それに対して、日本古
来の神道では神様は森羅万象、山や森の
木々等に宿ると考えます。祈りの対象は
自然そのもの、今歩み進んでいる参道の

urban oasis: Meiji Shrine, guarded by a forest of 170,000 trees. It is the rule of a shrine that the precincts and the approach are paved with **pure pebbles**, **rounded and polished like beads** by flowing water. From the dignified outer *torii* gateway, confirming the crunching sound of the pebbles as you proceed, you come to the main torii. Immediately to the right, several large trees spread their branches out majestically.

There are camphor trees, chinquapins, Japanese blue oaks, *shirakashi* (*Quercus myrsinaefolia*), and Japanese evergreen oaks. In a natural setting, these trees would never be found together. The reason they are here now, of course, is that the trees planted at the time of the shrine's construction have grown into a magnificent **shrine forest**. Almost 100 years ago, as many as 100,000 trees were donated from around the country, and it took seven years to plant them. Today the woodland looks perfectly natural and does not hint at having been artificially planted. It is a **crystallization** of the wisdom and relentless efforts of the Meiji people.

In Christian cathedrals, there is an image of Jesus Christ on a cross, and the ceiling is designed to symbolize the glorious world of God. People offer prayers to God up in heaven. By contrast, in Japan's ancient religion of Shinto, the gods **reside in mountains and trees** and **all of nature**. Prayers, therefore, are directed at nature itself. The trees that line the approach that you are walking along now are

柱の傷

両側にある森はすでに神の領域、神聖なる場です。清涼な空気を深呼吸し、味わってみてください。

ツリーウォッチングを楽しみながら本殿に進んでください。本殿手前の**外拝殿**の階段を上ったところで軒を支えている柱の傷に注目です。無数の傷は、本殿が再建された1958年から数年の間、**正月三が日**に押し寄せた300万人余の参拝者が遠くから投げ入れるお賽銭によってできたものです。

さてお参りが済んで、参道を戻って一の鳥居をくぐり境内から出ると、目の前には日本のシャンゼリゼ通りとも称せられる表参道が美しいけやき並木を見せて一直線に延びています。

原宿・表参道

その名前が示すようにこの道は明治神宮への参道として造られました。**元旦の初日の出**を東京で拝みたいと思ったら、JR上に架かる橋のあたりから表参道に向かって立ってみてください。この通りの真っすぐ先に初日の出が昇るはずです。明治神宮と自然がともにあることを実感できる一瞬です。

already a sacred place, the territory of the gods. Take a deep breath of fresh air and let it sink in.

While enjoying the trees, make your way to the main shrine. After climbing the steps in front of the main shrine to the **outer oratory**, you will notice the pockmarked pillars supporting the building. The countless dents come from the money thrown in from a distance by the 3 million or so worshippers who flocked to the temple on the **three-day New Year's holidays** during the years since 1958, when the main shrine was rebuilt.

After you finish worshipping at the shrine, return to the approach path and leave the shrine precincts through the outer torii. There, stretching in a straight line ahead of you, is Omotesando-dori, known as the Champs-Élysées of Tokyo and lined with beautiful zelkova trees.

Harajuku and Omotesando

As the name suggests, this avenue was built as the front approach to Meiji Shrine. (*Omote* means front and *sando* means approach.) If you want to see the **first sunrise on New Year's Day** in Tokyo, try standing on the bridge over the JR lines and looking in the Omotesando-dori direction. You should see the sun rising in the sky right in front of you. You see, Meiji Shrine and nature go together.

表参道周辺は今や日本随一のファッション最先端をゆくエリアです。海外のブランドのみならず、日本発の有名ブランド店も軒を並べています。世界に発信している日本ブランドの**旗艦店**をのぞいてみた後は、ぐっと趣を変えて、明治期の日本連合艦隊の旗艦「三笠」を率いてロシアのバルチック艦隊と戦ったアドミラル東郷のゆかりの地を訪ねてみましょう。

　海外でもその偉業が認められ、東洋のネルソンといわれたアドミラル東郷、日本帝国海軍元帥東郷平八郎です。明治通りと表参道の交差点を曲がり、竹下通り入り口あたりまで若者たちの喧騒にもまれながら進むと、その先左側に鳥居が見えてきます。鳥居とは**俗界**から神聖な場所へといざなう入り口ですが、まさにその意味の示す通り、一歩足を踏み入れると、目の前には池を取り囲むように広がる日本庭園です。あまりの静けさにタイムスリップしたかのようです。

　庭の中央にある「神池」に架かった橋を渡ると、みごとな**錦鯉**や緋鯉が寄ってきます。その先の階段を20段ほど上るとアドミラル東郷を祭る東郷神社の回廊が見えてきます。日本の国防には海軍の創設が必至と考えた若き日の東郷は、イ

The Omotesando vicinity is now one of the cutting-edge fashion areas in Japan. The streets are lined with shops selling both foreign brands and famous Japanese brands. After taking a peek inside the **flagship shops** of Japanese brands known throughout the world, let us turn back the clock and visit a place connected with Admiral Heihachiro Togo (1848–1934), who commanded the *Mikasa* — another flagship, this one of the Japanese imperial fleet in the Meiji Period — and fought against the Russian Baltic Fleet.

The feats of Admiral Togo were widely acknowledged not only in Japan but overseas as well, and he was nicknamed the "Nelson of the Orient." At the intersection of Omotesando-dori and Meiji-dori, coming from the station, turn left and, jostled by the crowds of young people in this area, walk as far as the entrance to Takeshita-dori. You will then see a torii on the left. A torii symbolically separates the **secular world** outside from the sacred world of the shrine within. And indeed, when you pass through the gateway, it is as if you step into another world, for there, stretching out in front of you, is a Japanese garden encircling a pond. The tranquility seems to take you back in time.

When you cross the bridge over the "sacred pond" in the center of the garden, many spectacular **brocade carp** and red carp gather below. Climbing the 20 or so steps in front of you, you will see the corridor of Togo Shrine, which is dedicated to Admiral Togo. Believing that the creation of a navy was essential for

ギリスへの7年間の留学中に英語、理科、**海軍学**は言うにおよばず、**国際法**まで学び、日露戦争では連合艦隊司令長官として活躍し、世界を驚かせました。

東郷神社
渋谷区神宮前1-5-3
03-3403-3591

　明治の二人の偉人を通じて近代日本の歴史にしばし触れる1日、いかがでしょうか。

太田記念美術館

　海外でも大人気の浮世絵を見たいなら、浮世絵専門の太田記念美術館もおすすめです。原宿の喧噪から一歩入った静かな一角に1万2000点にのぼる**収蔵**を誇る浮世絵専門美術館があります。原宿駅から表参道を進み、明治通りとの交差点一つ手前の角を左へ曲がるとすぐ左側に看板が見えてきます。

太田記念美術館
渋谷区神宮前1-10-
10
03-3403-0880
月曜定休（祝日の場合
は開館、翌日休館）

　庶民文化が花開いた江戸で愛読されたのは**木版画**印刷による書籍、瓦版、そして今でいうポスターのような浮世絵でした。かけそば1杯と同じ値段で、好きな役者の似顔絵、憧れの芸者の姿、**風刺画**などの浮世絵が買えたのです。また、固

the national defense of Japan, Togo in his younger days spent seven years studying in Britain, where he learned not only English, science, and **naval science** but also **international law**. Later, during the Russo-Japanese War of 1904–05, Togo amazed the world with his achievements as commander in chief of the Japanese Imperial Navy.

I hope you enjoyed this day of sightseeing, looking back at the history of modern Japan through these two great figures of the Meiji Period.

Ota Memorial Museum of Art

If you have a little more time and want to have a look at ukiyo-e paintings and prints, the nearby Ota Memorial Museum of Art, which specializes in this genre, is highly recommended. Just a short distance from the madding crowd of Harajuku, this quietly-situated museum boasts a **collection** of 12,000 ukiyo-e. Going from Harajuku Station along Omotesando-dori, you turn left at the corner just before the intersection with Meiji-dori. On the left you will see a sign pointing to the museum.

During the explosion of commoner culture in the city of Edo, popular reading consisted of **woodblock**-printed books, news-sheets, and, lastly, ukiyo-e prints, which might be considered the equivalent of modern posters. For the price of a bowl of soba noodles, you could buy a portrait of your favorite actor, a

い桜の木でできた版を使って大量に印刷
され、日本からヨーロッパへ輸出され
ていた陶器の**包装紙**となって海を渡り、
ゴッホをはじめとする当時の印象派の眼
にとまり、ジャポニズムの発端になった
ことは有名です。

　版元は総合プロデューサーです。題材
になる芸者や役者の着物のデザイン、小
物や持ち物を決め絵師に指示を出し流行
を作りました。江戸の人気商品はこのよ
うにして生まれていったのです。本物志
向の**日本びいき**のお客様には必ずおすす
めしているスポットです。

かまわぬ
渋谷区神宮1-10-10
太田記念美術館B1
03-3401-7957
月曜定休

　美術館の地下にあるかまわぬは手染め
のカラフルなデザインが楽しい手拭い専
門店。外国人には手拭いの使いみちを丁
寧に説明してくれます。特に人気のある
使い方は手拭いをスカーフにする、ある
いは別売りの木製のポールにかけて壁
掛けとして使うもの。手頃な値段で和の
アートが楽しめると評判です。

representation of a popular geisha, a **satirical piece**, or other types of ukiyo-e. The woodblocks were made of hard cherry wood and capable of producing prints in huge numbers. It is a well-known fact that these prints were used as **wrapping paper** for ceramics exported to Europe and were discovered by Impressionists like van Gogh, setting off the Japonisme fad.

The woodblock publishers, the *hanmoto*, were the brains behind the ukiyo-e. They decided the design of the kimonos worn by the actor or geisha figures, their accessories and other personal belongings, and passed this information on to the artists, in the process creating the fashions of the day. The most popular Edo faddish items came into being in this way. For hardcore **Japanophiles**, who are interested in the genuine article, this museum is highly recommended.

In the basement of the museum there is a pleasant tenugui (hand towel) shop called Kamawanu, which stocks hand-dyed towels of various colorful designs. The shop assistants will also explain ways of using a tenugui to foreigners. Especially popular methods are using tenugui as scarves or as wall decorations (the wooden poles on which they are hung are sold separately). This is a fun way of enjoying Japanese art at a reasonable price.

世界のAKIBA／秋葉原

Electronics Stores and Subcultures: Akihabara

for Ueno & Asakusa
上野・浅草方面 ↑

Suehirocho Station
末広町駅

Ginza Line
銀座線

Akiha
Dai Bui
秋
ダイ

Akky Main Store
Akky本店

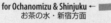

Kotobukiya Akihabara-kan
コトブキヤ秋葉原館

Electric Town Ex
電気街口

for Ochanomizu & Shinjuku ←
お茶の水・新宿方面

JR Sobu Line
JR 総武線

Laox Main Store
ラオックス本店

Akiha
Radio Ka
秋葉原ラジオ

Manseibashi
万世橋

Chuo-dori
中央通り

for Ochanomizu
御茶ノ水方面

for Ginza & Shibuya ↓
銀座・渋谷方面

JR Chuo Line
JR 中央線

N

for Ka
神田

↑ **for Ueno & Ikebukuro**
上野・池袋方面

↑ **for Ueno**
上野方面

Kuramaebashi-dori
蔵前橋通り

↑ **for Tsukuba**
筑波方面

JR Yamanote Line
JR 山手線

Tsukuba Express (Subway)
つくばエクスプレス

Hibiya Line
日比谷線

abara

ding
葉原
ス
ノ

Akihabara Station
秋葉原駅

Yodobashi Akiba
ヨドバシアキバ

Akihabara Station
秋葉原駅

Akihabara Station
秋葉原駅

→ **for Kinshi-cho & Chiba**
錦糸町・千葉方面

↓ **for Ginza**
銀座方面

Kandagawa River
神田川

or Kanda & Tokyo
神田・東京方面

秋葉原

　日本の首都、東京には今や世界のトップブランドが集まり、お金さえあれば何でも手に入ります。中でも、**電化製品を**お探しの方ならどうしても訪ねたいのが、**親しみを込めて**アキバとも呼ばれる秋葉原の街です。今や世界中に知られる日本の電化製品、IT機器を買うなら、ここはまさにパラダイスといえるでしょう。日本国内では、大型量販店やインターネットの普及で秋葉原でなければ手に入らない電化製品は減ってきましたが、勝手を知らない外国人にとっては、すべてが揃っている秋葉原は、なくてはならない場所なのです。

　訪れる外国人の数もうなぎ上りです。その買い物風景はお国柄が出るようです。アメリカ人は思ったよりは値段が安くないことに不満をもらしながら日本でしか買えない新製品を見つけてご満悦。ヨーロッパからのお客様は自国より安い値段のついた商品を見つけては**熱心に品定め**。アジアの方々はさまざまな家電製品を、両手に持ちきれないほどお買い物です。

　秋葉原の歴史は日本の戦後から現代にいたる高度経済成長、技術の進歩に対応

Akihabara

Nowadays the world's top brands have all come to Tokyo, the capital of Japan, and as long as you have the money, you can buy anything you want. If it is **electric appliances** you are looking for, there is one place that you really must visit — Akihabara, or "Akiba" as it is **affectionately** known. Akihabara is a paradise for electric goods and information technology equipment that has gained an international reputation in recent years. In Japan itself, as a result of the emergence of large discount stores elsewhere and the diffusion of the Internet, the number of electric goods that can be obtained only in Akihabara has declined. But for foreigners who do not know their way around, Akihabara is a must because it has, well, just about everything.

The number of foreigners visiting "Akiba" is increasing rapidly, and their manner of shopping often reveals where they are from. Americans tend to be disgruntled that prices are not as cheap as they had expected but then gleeful when they find a new product that can only be purchased in Japan. Europeans eagerly look for products that are cheaper than in their own country and **scrutinize** them. Asians go on buying sprees and can be seen struggling away with armfuls of shopping bags.

From the postwar period to the present, the history of Akihabara has evolved almost on a daily

して取扱商品を変化させ進化してきた、発展の日々そのものです。1950年代のラジオ部品の**店頭販売**から始まり、60年代の家電製品専門店街、90年代はパソコン普及に伴って本体と周辺機器の販売、その後2000年代のアニメ、コミック漫画から生まれたフィギュア、コスプレなどのポップカルチャーの時代と変わり続けてきました。

そして、今や、秋葉原の新時代を**牽引している**のはオタクと呼ばれる、知識力が高く審美眼もあるプロ消費者です。ネガティブなイメージは昔のこと。あのスティーブ・ジョブズもれっきとした時代の先の先を目指したオタクだったともいえるのですから。

コスプレ喫茶が発展してお客様をご主人様、お嬢様と呼んでもてなし、癒してくれるメイドカフェも秋葉原名物です。現代版**お座敷遊び**です。彼らがプロなら、あなたもお客様に徹して"もてなされ上手"にならなければいけません。

JR秋葉原駅の土日の乗降客は50万人を超えます。駅に降り立ったら、あわてずにプラットフォームや通路にある電気街口、あるいは英語「Electric Town」の表示に従って無事に改札口に到着します。地下鉄なら銀座線「末広町駅」、あるいは日比谷線「秋葉原駅」が最寄りとな

basis, keeping pace with the high-growth period and technological developments by changing the products offered. Akihabara began with the **storefront sales** of radio parts in the 1950s, preceded to electric appliances sold in specialty shops in the 1960s, then to computers and accessories in the 1990s, and finally in the 2000s to pop culture in the form of figurines, cosplay, and so on that emerged from anime and manga.

And now, the **driving force** behind Akihabara is provided by the *otaku*, who are in effect highly intelligent, aesthetically inclined professional consumers. The old negative otaku image has faded away. In fact, you can say that Steve Jobs himself was a farsighted otaku.

Cosplay cafes developed into maid cafes, which are a particular feature of Akihabara. Here the customer plays the role of the master of the house and the waitress that of the maid, whose role is to make the master feel at ease. It is a kind of modern **parlor game**. If the maids are professionals in providing hospitality, you must be a professional in being hospitalitized.

On Saturdays the JR Akihabara Station is used by more than 500,000 people. Disembarking from the train, there is no need to get confused; just follow the signs on the platform and corridors in Japanese or English that say Electric Town and you will safely reach the exit. If you are taking a subway, the Suehiro Station on the Ginza Line or the Akihabara Station on

ヨドバシAkiba
千代田区神田花岡町
1-1
03-5209-1010
無休

ラオックス秋葉原本店
千代田区外神田
1-2-9
03-3253-7111
無休

AKKY本店
千代田区外神田
1-12-1
03-5207-5027
無休

ります。

まずはJRの改札口を左へ出てください。左を見ると東西自由通路と書かれた通路が見えます。そこを通りぬけたらまた左へ。目の前にヨドバシカメラの**目立つ建物**が見えてきます。2005年に開店以来、人の流れを変えたとまでいわれています。電化製品に加えて、マッサージ店やゴルフ専門店までそろったショッピングセンターです。最上階のレストラン街も世界中の料理が楽しめる充実ぶりです。ここだけで圧倒され満足してしまうお客様も多いのですが、ここからが**ガイドの腕のみせどころ**です。秋葉原の原点そして日々進化するアキバの魅力探訪トリップはここからです。

元気を出して東西自由通路に戻り、女性に喜ばれるカフェなどのある駅ビルアトレ1を右に見ながら中央通り方面へす

JR線高架下の中央通り

the Hibiya Line are the most convenient.

First of all, leaving the JR exit, turn to the left. Looking again to the left, you will see a corridor that says East West Passage. Emerging from this corridor, you go to the left once more. Immediately in front of you, you see the quite **conspicuous** Yodobashi Camera building. Since its opening in 2005, it is said to have actually changed the flow of pedestrian traffic. In addition to electric appliances, this shopping center boasts everything from massage parlors to golf shops. The restaurant area on the top floor also offers a wide variety of cuisines from around the world. There are some overwhelmed visitors who are completely satisfied at this point, but in fact this is where the **tour guide shows her mettle**. It is from here that the real meaning of continually evolving "Akiba" is discovered and the real adventure begins.

Recovering our spirits, we return to the East West Passage and head for Chuo-dori, with the station building's Atre 1 on our right, where there are a good

アニメやメイドの
店が立ち並ぶ

すみます。

秋葉原の魅力は古いものと新しいものが**重層的**に存在していることにあります。戦後のようすを彷彿とさせる原点といえば、JR線高架下にあるラジオストアー（2013年に閉館）、ラジオセンター、電波会館の3つがつながった建物です。**迷路のような細い通路**が走っています。数えきれないほどの商店がカウンターひとつだけで商売を繰り広げています。ラジオ部品販売に始まり電子部品、カメラ、工具、イルミネーションライト、発車ベルスイッチ、金属探知機、半導体などありとあらゆる部品の宝庫です。技術と知識があれば7000円程度ここで部品を買い揃えればPC1台の組み立ても可能だそうです。ここでは**電気で動くものはなんでも**手にはいります。

さて電気製品からはなれて、中央通りに戻りましょう。緑色の高架線に沿って中央通りを横切り、そのまま細い道を線路と平行に直進し、一つ目の角を右に曲がると、お待ちかねのオタクの**聖地**、クールジャパンのメッカ、ロボットやフィギュアの専門店が目の前に広がります。メイドカフェのPR・呼び込みメイドさんもあなたを笑顔で迎えてくれるでしょう。路上でのメイドさんの写真撮影はご法度なのでご注意ください。彼女らは肖

秋葉原ラジオセンター
千代田区外神田
1-14-2
03-3251-0614

秋葉原電波会館
千代田区外神田
1-14-3

秋葉原ラジオ会館
千代田区外神田
1-15-16

さまざまな衣裳を楽しむ若者たち

number of cafes that are particularly popular among female visitors.

One of the greatest appeals of Akihabara is the **overlapping strata** of old and new. The spot that is most reminiscent of the postwar period is the building under the JR elevated railway which has the Radio Store (closed in 2013), the Radio Center, and the Radio Wave Hall, all in a line. Going down a narrow, **mazelike corridor**, each of the shops has a single counter that is overflowing with products for sale. These shops started out selling radio parts but now they offer a virtual treasure trove of components for various objects: electronics, cameras, tools, illumination lights, train platform buzzer switches, metal detectors, and semiconductors. I am told that if you have the technical expertise and practical knowhow, you can buy all the parts needed to build a personal computer for around ¥7,000. **Anything that moves by electricity** can be purchased here.

Tearing ourselves away from the electric parts, let's return to Chuo-dori. Crossing the street, which runs along the green elevated train line, and going straight down a narrow road parallel to the tracks, you turn right at the first corner. Here you find yourself in the **sacred land** of the otaku, the Mecca of Cool Japan, with specialty shops dealing in robots and figurines spread out before you. There will be maids out touting their particular maid cafes, greeting you with friendly smiles. Note that taking their photos here is verboten. After all, they are a professional group with the legal

像権を持っているプロ集団です。

この通りの先、左側にホビーショップの**老舗**「コトブキヤ」で、日本のサブカルチャーの双璧であるアニメとコミックスのヒーロー、ヒロインのフィギュアを見ていただきたいものです。その**精巧な**仕上がりを一目見れば人気の秘密がわかります。マンガ本やアニメなど2次元の憧れの主人公たちが3次元になって目の前であなたをみつめているのです。手足や胴体もあなたの好きなように動かしてポーズを変えることもできるものもあります。もしかしたら**はまってしまう**かもしれません。

モノづくりの最先端技術の宝庫の街、秋葉原はオタクだけの世界にしていてはもったいないのです。なぜか入ってゆくのに勇気のいるところばかりですが、一歩を踏み出せば楽しい世界が待っています。

コトブキヤ秋葉原館
千代田区外神田1-8-8
03-5298-6300
無休

アニメ、コミックなどのフィギュアが並ぶ

rights to their own portraits.

Further down this street, on the left side, you see the main store of the **venerable** hobby **shop** Kotobukiya. Here I would like you to see for yourself the figurines of the heroes and heroines of Japanese manga and anime, the family jewels of subculture Japan. Just one glance at their **intricate** construction will reveal the secret behind their popularity. The two-dimensional protagonists of manga and anime have been transformed into three-dimensional figures that return your steady gaze. With some, the body, arms and legs can be arranged as you wish and new poses can be created. Be careful—you could **become addicted**.

At the cutting edge of Japanese craftsmanship and technology, Akihabara should not be left exclusively in the hands of the otaku. For some reason it takes a little courage to enter this special sphere, but once you have taken the first step, a world of delight awaits you.

for Aoyama 1-chome ↑
青山一丁目方面

Nogizaka Station
乃木坂駅

National Art Center
国立新美術館

for Meijijingumae & Yoyogi Uehara
明治神宮前・代々木上原方面

Chiyoda Line
千代田線

Roppongi Tunnel
六本木トンネル

Roppongi Sta
六本木駅

Hibiya Line
日比谷線

● **Roppongi Hills Tower**
六本木ヒルズタワー

Roppongi Hills
六本木ヒルズ

Keyakizaka-dori
けやき坂通り

Azabu-Juban Shopp
麻布十番商店街

Kurayamizaka Slo
暗闇坂

Blue and Whi
ブルー&ホワ

N

for Meguro & Hiyos
目黒・日吉方面

→ **for Nijubashimae & Ayase**
二重橋前・綾瀬方面

Suntory Museum of Art
サントリー美術館

Tokyo Midtown
東京ミッドタウン

oppongi Station
本木駅

Roppongi-dori
六本木通り

Hibiya Line
日比谷線

Gaienhigashi-dori
外苑東通り

for Kasumigaseki
霞ヶ関方面

現代アートと
トレンドの街・六本木
Modern Art and the Latest Trends:
Roppongi

izaka-shita
坂下

Toei Oedo Line
営大江戸線

↑ **for Ichigaya & Urawamisono**
市ヶ谷・浦和美園方面

amegen
源

Azabu-Juban Station
麻布十番駅

↘ **for Daimon & Ryogoku**
大門・両国方面

anboku Line
南北線

六本木

このエリアを歩くと外国人の多さに
びっくりです。東京の中にあるもっとも
国際色あふれる街、それが六本木です。
東京にある130余りの大使館の半分以上
がこの界隈に集っています。とはいえ江
戸の頃は多くの寺と大名屋敷のある坂の
多い一帯でした。暗闇坂、狸穴などの地
名からも想像できる静かなところだった
のが、今や話題の新名所と不夜城・歓楽
街で世界にその名を知られるようになり
ました。

暗闇坂

暗闇坂は、港区麻布十
番2丁目から元麻布3
丁目に向かって上る坂
で、当時は木がうっそ
うと茂り、昼間でも暗
かった。同じく麻布台
2丁目あたりを江戸初
期には狸穴と呼んだ。
この地にアナグマが
生息していたらしい。

　ツアーで体験した六本木の夜をご紹介
しましょう。韓国への正式訪問を控えて、
お忍びで日本に立ち寄った中東のとある
国の皇太子は六本木のカラオケバーに行
きたいとのこと。VIPルームにお座りに
なったままでしたが、同行したガイドで
ある私に歌をご所望されました。カーペ
ンターズとダイアナ・ロスの2曲を披露
させていただきました。皇太子に褒めて
いただいたこの2曲は今でも得意のマイ
ソングです。

　2002年日韓共催のワールドサッカーで
デビッド・ベッカム率いるイングランド
チームを応援するために訪日したサポー

Roppongi

The first thing to strike you about this area of Tokyo is the large number of foreigners on the streets. Roppongi is the most cosmopolitan place in Tokyo. **More than half of the 130 or so foreign embassies** in Tokyo are located in this neighborhood. Of course, it was not always like this. In the Edo Period it was an area of temples, slopes, and daimyo mansions. Surviving place names like Kurayamizaka ("pitch dark hill") and Mamiana ("badger hole") attest to how quiet it must have been. But now Roppongi has gained an international reputation as a sleepless entertainment district and a place with some popular new tourist spots.

Let me tell you about an evening that I once spent in Roppongi. Ahead of an official visit to South Korea, a crown prince from a certain country in the Middle East visited Japan **incognito** and said that he wanted to go to a karaoke bar in Roppongi. The crown prince just remained seated in the bar's VIP room, but he requested me, his guide, to get up and sing. I performed two songs, one by the Carpenters and the other by Diana Ross. The crown prince praised my singing, and now those two songs are my standards whenever I go to a karaoke bar.

During the 2002 FIFA World Cup, which was cohosted by Japan and South Korea, supporters of the David Beckham–led England team who had come

ターツアーの面々は、カラオケルームで夜中の3時過ぎまで、テーブルに上がってダンスに歌にと勝利を祝うパーティーで大騒ぎ。チームが勝ち続ける間はサポーターも応援のために北海道から茨城と転々と追っかけをしていました。ところがイングランドチームが**準々決勝**でブラジルに負けた静岡スタジアムですべては終わりました。サポーターを乗せた大型バスは夜中の東名高速をひた走り、東京のホテルへ着いたのは午前2時近く。翌日には帰国の途につかれたのでした。

六本木の夜を楽しんだ翌日は、集合時間に遅刻、あるいは二日酔いでツアーを欠席する人もたまにいます。**モーニングコール**などまるで効果なく、ドアを叩いてもまだ目を覚まさない御仁には、ホテルのマネージャーがマスターキーでドアを開ける強行手段に出ることもたまにあります。六本木にまつわる夜の思い出には事欠きません。

夜の顔とはまったく違った新たな魅力ある新名所も加わりました。**再開発**により誕生した六本木ヒルズと東京ミッドタウンです。その建物群の最新のデザイン、天空にある美術館、波打つガラスの美術館、路上や建物内で観賞できる海外著名作家によるアートの数々、**グルメをうならせる**有名ステーキレストランやセレブ御用達の高級居酒屋、炉ばた焼きの店な

to Japan for the tournament used to hold parties in karaoke rooms in Roppongi until 3 o'clock in the morning, standing on the tables to dance, sing, and celebrate their team's victories. The supporters traveled from Hokkaido to Ibaraki to see the matches. For the England team, the tournament ended in Shizuoka, when they lost to Brazil in the **quarter-finals**. The despondent England supporters traveled back to Tokyo by bus along the Tomei Expressway, reaching their hotel at nearly two in the morning. The next day they headed for home.

After a night out in Roppongi, visitors are often late for their assembly times the next morning or occasionally have to miss tours altogether because of hangovers. **Wake-up calls** have no effect whatsoever, and knocks on the door go unanswered. On occasions I have even had to ask the hotel manager to open the guest's door with a master key. Yes, I have many memories of evenings spent in Roppongi.

Several attractive new spots have appeared in Roppongi that are completely different from its night-life image. The **redevelopment** there has given birth to Roppongi Hills and Tokyo Midtown. They feature innovative architectural designs, a sky-high art museum, a wavy glass art center, a steak restaurant that will **make gourmets ooh and aah**, high-class drinking establishments favored by celebrities, and outdoor and indoor works of art by internationally

ど、何度でも訪れたくなる魅力満載の地区として注目されています。

国立新美術館

国立新美術館
港区六本木7-22-2
03-5777-8600
火曜定休
（火曜が祝日の場合は
開館、翌日休み）

千代田線乃木坂駅に直結していて0分。そこは**波がうねるような**曲線を描くガラスの壁が印象的な日本で5番目の国立の美術館、国立新美術館です。**自然との共生**を提唱した建築家・黒川紀章のデザインです。建物の内部へ入りましょう。透明なガラスのカーテンのようにゆらめく壁越しに眺められる前庭の景観の広がりは圧巻です。まるで森の中にいるような感覚です。新しい視点でさまざまな企画を立て、主に現代美術を発信してゆく美術館です。建物の斬新さ、充実したミュージアムショップも魅力的です。

東京ミッドタウン

国立新美術館を出て左へ3分ほど歩くと東京ミッドタウンです。**旧防衛庁跡地**に高さ248メートル、54階建のミッドタワーを含めて5棟の建物、敷地の40％を占めるオープンスペースには芝の広場が

renowned artists. These places are so full of attractions and surprises, you can visit them many times and never get bored.

National Art Center, Tokyo

Directly connected to Nogizaka Station on the Chiyoda Line (0 minutes away) is the National Art Center, Tokyo, the fifth national art museum in Japan, with its impressive curved glass wall that **resembles undulating waves**. The center was designed by the architect Kisho Kurokawa, who advocated **symbiosis with nature**. Let's go inside. The spacious atrium, which can be seen through the glass wall that seems to be swaying like a curtain, is truly awesome. It really does feel just like being in a forest. The National Art Center presents various special exhibitions from new perspectives and shows mainly modern art. As well as the novelty of the building itself, the well-stocked museum shop is an attraction, too.

Tokyo Midtown

Leaving the National Art Center, walk about three minutes to the left and you will reach Tokyo Midtown. Built on the **site of the former Defense Agency**, this complex of five buildings, including the 248-meter-high, 54-floor Midtown Tower, and the Green Square

憩いの場を提供しています。基本デザインはアメリカのスキッドモア・オーウィングズ・アンド・メリル社（Skidmore, Owings & Merrill, 略称 SOM）。ニューヨークのグラウンドゼロのフリーダムタワーを手がけたアメリカ大手建築事務所です。

サントリー美術館
港区赤坂9-7-4
東京ミッドタウン
ガレリア3F
03-3479-8600
火曜定休

　向かって左側に建つガレリアの中、3階にサントリー美術館の入り口があります。国宝を含む日本の古美術約3000点を収蔵しています。テーマ毎に展示を変えているので、蒔絵、絵画、陶磁器、ガラス、版画など、日本美術好きな方にはうれしい発見に巡り合える、何度訪れても楽しめる美術館です。館内の6階にはお茶室玄鳥庵があり、月に2回、木曜日にはお手前を楽しみながら**抹茶**がいただ

箸長
港区赤坂9-7-4
東京ミッドタウン
ガレリア3F
03-5413-0392
元日のみ休み

けます。同じくガレリア3階のお箸専門店箸長では、しゃれたケースに入った**環境に優しい**持ち歩き専用のマイ箸などいかがでしょうか。高級品を扱っている店舗やレストランが目立つ複合商業施設ですが、分かりやすいレイアウトです。ゆったりとした通路を歩けば、都会で味わう極上の生活に必要なものが見つかること受合いです。

and garden (open space accounts for 40 percent of Tokyo Midtown's area) provide both recreation and relaxation. The basic design was done by Skidmore, Owings & Merrill, a leading US architectural office that has designed the Freedom Tower for the "ground zero" site of the former World Trade Center in New York.

On the third floor of the Galleria building to your left is the entrance to the Suntory Museum of Art, which has about 3,000 antiques, including national treasures. The museum changes its exhibits in accordance with various themes, so Japanese art lovers will be delighted to discover gold lacquer art, paintings, ceramics, glass, prints, etc. It is a museum that can be visited again and again. On the 6th floor of the museum, there is a teahouse, Gencho-an, where you can enjoy **a cup of green tea** with a tea ceremony on Thursdays twice a month. Also on the third floor is the chopstick specialty store Hashicho, where you can buy your own **environmentally friendly** chopsticks in a stylish case. Although there are countless high-class shops and restaurants in this commercial complex, the layout is very easy to understand. If you walk leisurely along the corridors, you are sure to find what you need for high-quality living in the city.

六本木ヒルズ

六本木ヒルズ

　東京ミッドタウンから六本木交差点を目指し、右へ曲がって左側、薄い水色に輝く森ビルが見えてきます。200以上のお店、ホテル、住居、映画館、テレビ局、日本庭園、美術館などが集った**複合商業施設の草分け**的存在の六本木ヒルズです。ここ六本木6丁目はゆるやかに下る何本かの坂の周りに金魚屋さんなど数百の家々が集まっていた庶民の住宅地でした。17年を経て全住民が立ち退き、その12ヘクタール弱の空間に登場した東京の新名所です。

　開業して3日目にグループを案内した筆者は、あまりの複雑な建物の配置に、思わず案内の専門ガイドさんになぜこのように分かり難いのかと尋ねたのです。すると答えは、迷ってしまったと不安になったときにふと出合うショップや風景を楽しむ、**かくれんぼ**のドキドキを味わっていただきたいからとのこと。読者の皆様もしっかりと迷って、思ってもみなかったスポットの発見を楽しんでください。
　母への憧れを表した20個の白い卵を抱く蜘蛛の彫刻「ママン」をはじめ20余りあるパブリックアートを発見するのも六本木ヒルズの楽しみのひとつです。おす

Roppongi Hills

From Tokyo Midtown walk to the Roppongi crossing and turn right. Eventually, on your left, the light blue Mori Building will come into view. This is Roppongi Hills, a **pioneering commercial complex** with more than 200 shops, a hotel, residences, a cinema, a television station, a Japanese landscape garden, an art museum, and other attractions. This area, Roppongi 6-chome, used to be a residential district where ordinary folk, including goldfish vendors, lived in hundreds of dwellings built around the several gently sloping hills. Over 17 years all of the residents moved out of their homes, and one of Tokyo's newest attractions was built on a space of nearly 12 hectares.

On the third day after the opening of Roppongi Hills in 2003, when I was showing a group around the complex, I was so confused by the layout that I asked one of the information guides on duty why it was so difficult to understand. The reply was that it is like the thrill of a game of **hide-and-seek**: Just when you get lost and start feeling anxious, you come across a shop or spectacle that really delights you. So readers, don't worry if you get lost in Roppongi Hills; there is sure to be an unexpected surprise around the corner.

Another delight at Roppongi Hills is discovering the 20 or so works of public art, such as the *Maman* sculpture showing a spider embracing 20 white eggs — an expression of the sculptor's love for his

すめは遠方に東京タワーを借景として凛と立つ赤いバラのオブジェです。蜘蛛の彫刻のすぐ近くにあります。

　中央にそびえる森ビルの53階には天空の美術館と称される森美術館があります。52階には海抜250メートルから東京を360度見渡せる東京シティビューがあります。1300万人が住む東京の絶景を堪能してください。夜間と昼間の人口の差は300万人。周辺の都市を含むと3000万人近くが住む東洋一のメガロポリスです。東京タワーが手にとるように近くに見え、季節に合わせて色を微妙に変えるレインボーブリッジの先には未来都市のような**臨海副都心**が広がります。変わりゆく東京を実感する展望フロアです。住む、働く、遊ぶ、学ぶのすべてがかなう、小さな、しかし完璧な街がここにあります。災害時には、逃げ出すビルではなく逃げ込むビルになるという強い決意を表すように、森ビルの地下には**備蓄倉庫**もあり、六本木ヒルズ全体で約5000人を受け入れられる体制を整えてあるのです。

森美術館
港区六本木6-10-1
六本木ヒルズ
森タワー53階
03-5777-8600

東京シティビュー
港区六本木6-10-1
六本木ヒルズ
森タワー52階
03-6406-6652

麻布十番

　六本木ヒルズは坂の斜面に建設された

mother. I also recommend the red rose sculpture standing elegantly nearby, with Tokyo Tower in the background.

The Mori Building, which rises in the center of Roppongi Hills, has the Mori Museum of Art on the 53rd floor. One floor below, Tokyo City View, which is situated 250 meters above sea level, offers a wonderful panoramic view of Tokyo, a sprawling city with 13 million residents. The difference between the daytime and nighttime population of Tokyo is as many as 3 million persons. If the surrounding areas are included, the resident population of Tokyo and its vicinity soars to nearly 30 million, making it the largest megalopolis in the East. Tokyo Tower seems to be very close indeed, and beyond Rainbow Bridge, which changes color to match the season, the **waterfront subcenter of Tokyo** appears like a futuristic city. The view from this observation floor really does make you aware of how Tokyo is changing. The Mori Building is a small yet perfect town where you can live, work, play, and learn. It is determined to be, in the event of a disaster, a building that you can escape to, rather than escape from. It has a **stockpile of supplies** in the basement, and the entire Roppongi Hills complex is prepared to accommodate about 5,000 people.

Azabu-Juban

Since Roppongi Hills is built on inclining land,

ので、中央を通り抜けるけやき坂通りは400メートルのなだらかな坂になっています。坂の所々に小さい水平な場所があります。高齢者や車椅子の方へのやさしいバリアフリーの休憩の場になっています。この坂を下り切って交差点を右へ曲がり、一の橋方面へ歩き、すぐに右へ斜めに入る狭い道に進みます。麻布十番商店街です。ベーカリー、スーパー、花屋、雑貨屋、魚屋、食器屋などなど、庶民が毎日買い物に訪れます。ここは皇居から直線で2.6キロほどしか離れていません。都心のホテルに滞在中、**庶民の暮らしぶり**を見たいという外国の方には最適な商店街です。

左側にあるお豆とおかきの専門店、創業慶應元年（1865年）の豆源に立ち寄り、麻布十番商店街のいち押しお土産を買ったら、その十字路を左へ曲がり、1分歩いてみてください。すると、2メートルの高低差のある坂道にできた、この商店街のオアシス的緑地、パティオ十番とよばれる広場にでます。6本のケヤキを見上げながら、ここで一休みです。さて、小さな少女の像も見逃せません。1902年に生まれ、この近くにあった孤児院で9歳で亡くなったきみちゃんです。この女の子は、童謡「赤い靴」のモデルと言われています。アメリカ人宣教師の養女になり横浜港からどこかへ行ってしまったと

豆源
港区麻布十番1-8-12
03-3583-0962
火曜不定休

Keyakizaka-dori, which runs through the center, is a 400-meter gently sloping hill. Along this slope there are several small horizontal spaces that serve as barrier-free resting places for the elderly and wheelchair users. Go down this hill, turn right at the intersection, and walk in the direction of Ichinohashi. You will soon see a narrow road leading diagonally to the right. This is the Azabu-Juban shopping street, where ordinary people living in the vicinity do their daily shopping. There are bakeries, supermarkets, florists, general stores, fishmongers, tableware shops, and so on and so forth. As the crow flies, this shopping street is just 2.6 kilometers from the Imperial Palace. It is an ideal place for foreigners staying in grand hotels in central Tokyo to get out and see **how the ordinary Japanese live**.

Stop by Mamegen, the bean and Japanese rice cracker specialty store on the left. It was founded in 1865, and you can buy the Azabu Juban shopping street's best souvenirs there. Then, turn left at the crossroads and walk for one minute. You will come to a plaza called Patio-Juban, a green oasis in this shopping district, which is formed from a slope with a height difference of 2 meters. Take a break here, looking up at the six zelkova trees. Do not miss the statue of a little girl, Kimi, who was born in 1902 and died at the age of nine in an orphanage near here. It's said that the Japanese nursery rhyme "The Red Shoes" is based on her. In the song, she was adopted by an American missionary and left Japan via the port of Yokohama, but there is a theory that

歌われていますが、実際は、病気のために渡米できず、この近くの孤児院で亡くなったという説があり、**記念像**が建てられました。

さて、元気がでたら、きみちゃんの像を背にして、目の前の道をまっすぐ進み、1つ目の左側角の屋外エスカレーターで2階に上ると、藍染工芸品や和物の専門店Blue and White があります。合わせて10人の子供を持つ3人の女性が**日本の伝統美**に目覚め、それを伝えたいと和の工芸品のみを扱うお店を1975年に始めました。周辺の大使館の在日外交官に絶大な人気があり、大使夫人もよく訪れるとのことです。

十番商店街からは徒歩3分ほどで地下鉄南北線、大江戸線の麻布十番駅です。毎年、8月の終わりには、周辺は麻布十番納涼祭りでにぎわいます。六本木から麻布十番エリアは、アクセスも便利になった東京の新名所です。

Blue and White
港区麻布十番2-9-2
03-3451-0537
火曜・祝日定休

she actually died in an orphanage near here because an illness prevented her from going to the US, and a **commemorative statue** was built for her.

If you are feeling energetic, face away from the Kimi-chan monument, go straight down the street in front of you, and take the first outdoor escalator on your left to the second floor, where you will find Blue and White, a store specializing in indigo-dyed crafts and Japanese goods. This shop was started in 1975 by three women (the mothers of a total of 10 children) who became aware of the **beauty of Japanese tradition** and wanted to transmit it to others. Blue and White is immensely popular among foreign diplomats working at embassies in the vicinity, and apparently the wives of ambassadors are frequent customers.

A walk of about three minutes from the Azabu-Juban shopping district brings you to Azabu-Juban Station on the Namboku and Oedo subway lines. The Azabu-Juban summer festival is held at the end of August every year. The Roppongi–Azabu-Juban area is one of Tokyo's popular new spots, and it has convenient transportation access.

日本のシンボル・皇居

The Symbol of Japan: The Imperial Palace

for Nakano & Kudanshita ↑
中野・九段下方面

Nippon Budokan
日本武道館

Kitanomaru Park
北の丸公園

Daikancho
代官町

Edo Castle Site
天守閣跡

Fukiage Gosho
吹上御所

Imperial Palace
皇居

Sakashitamor
坩

Gosho
御所

Hanzomon Gate
半蔵門

New Kyuden
新宮殿

Sanden State Hall
宮中三殿

Fushimi Yagura
伏見櫓

Imperial Household Agency
宮内庁庁舎

Nijubashi Brid
二重橋

Sakuradamon Gate
桜田門

Sakuradamon Station
桜田門駅

Uchibori
内堀通

for Nagatacho & Ikebukuro ←
永田町・池袋方面

National Diet Building
国会議事堂

Kasumigaseki
霞ヶ関

for Nogizaka & Yoyogi Uehara
乃木坂・代々木上原方面

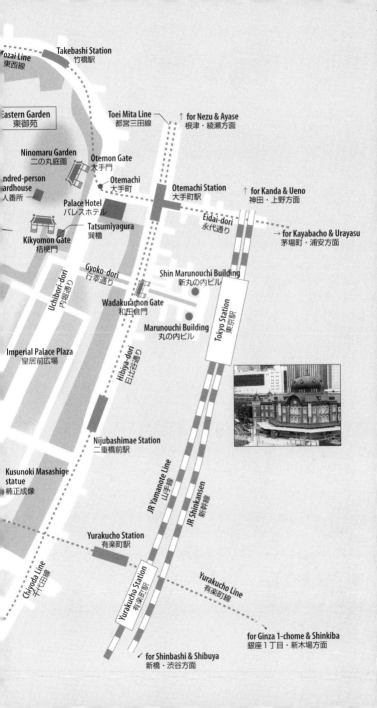

ozai Line
東西線

Takebashi Station
竹橋駅

Eastern Garden
東御苑

Toei Mita Line
都営三田線

↑ for Nezu & Ayase
根津・綾瀬方面

Ninomaru Garden
二の丸庭園

Otemon Gate
大手門

ndred-person
ardhouse
百人番所

Otemachi
大手町

Otemachi Station
大手町駅

↑ for Kanda & Ueno
神田・上野方面

Palace Hotel
パレスホテル

Eidai-dori
永代通り

→ for Kayabacho & Urayasu
茅場町・浦安方面

Tatsumiyagura
巽櫓

Kikyomon Gate
桔梗門

Gyoko-dori
行幸通り

Shin Marunouchi Building
新丸の内ビル

Uchibori-dori
内堀通り

Wadakuramon Gate
和田倉門

Tokyo Station
東京駅

Marunouchi Building
丸の内ビル

Imperial Palace Plaza
皇居前広場

Hibiya-dori
日比谷通り

Nijubashimae Station
二重橋前駅

Kusunoki Masashige
statue
楠正成像

JR Yamanote Line
山手線

JR Shinkansen
新幹線

Chiyoda Line
千代田線

Yurakucho Station
有楽町駅

Yurakucho Station
有楽町駅

Yurakucho Line
有楽町線

for Ginza 1-chome & Shinkiba
銀座1丁目・新木場方面

✓ for Shinbashi & Shibuya
新橋・渋谷方面

皇居

皇居
千代田区千代田1-1
03-5223-8071 (宮
内庁管理部参観係)
＊参観には事前申し
込みが必要。

皇居とは天皇がかかわるさまざまな公的行事が行われる新宮殿、天皇皇后両陛下の御住まいの吹上仙洞御所、皇室の重要な儀式が行われる宮中三殿、宮内庁庁舎、皇宮警察本部などがある地域の総称です。北には科学技術館やビートルズの日本初公演で有名になった武道館がある北の丸公園。一般公開している東御苑は**その名の通り**東側に広がります。南にはいつもハイスピードで通り過ぎる車やバスで混雑している内堀通りが東京タワーに向かって一直線に伸びています。

皇居の周囲約5キロのゆるやかな起伏に富む歩道からはお堀と石垣、芝が植えられた土塁、豊かな森が眺められます。都内随一ののびやかな気分が味わえる景観です。このコースには皇居への出入りに使用される数箇所の門がありますが、**信号はひとつもありません。**というわけでジョギングにはもってこい。**日本のど真ん中**で皇居の景色を楽しみながらのランニングです。半蔵門から走り始める人が多いのは、この近辺に、着替え室、ロッ

The Imperial Palace

The Imperial Palace is the name given to an area that houses several facilities, including the new Kyuden, where official events involving the Emperor are carried out; Fukiage Sento Palace the residence of the Emperor and Empress; the Sanden State Hall, where important ceremonies of the imperial family are conducted; the Imperial Household Agency; and the Imperial Guard Headquarters. On the northern side there is Kitanomaru Park, which includes the Science Museum and the Nippon Budokan concert hall, where the Beatles famously played in 1966. Higashi Gyoen (Eastern Garden), which is open to the public, is situated, **as its name suggests**, on the eastern side of the palace. On the southern side, Uchibori-dori, which is always busy with fast-moving traffic, runs straight toward Tokyo Tower.

From the gently-sloping sidewalk around the Imperial Palace, which extends for about five kilometers, you can see moats, stone walls, earthwork now covered with grass, and lush woodland. It is without doubt the most relaxing spot in Tokyo. Along the pathway there are gates in several places, used for entering and leaving the Imperial Palace, but **there are no traffic lights at all**. It is, therefore, an ideal course for jogging. It is a run where you can enjoy views of the Imperial Palace, the **very heart of Japan**. Many people start running from Hanzomon because there are

カー完備の銭湯や貸出ランニングウェアー完備のスポーツ施設などがあるからです。**手ぶらで来ても即楽しめる**、皇居マラソンは、まさにランナーの聖地！ 休日にはマラソン大会もよく行われます。緑豊かな約115万平方メートルの皇居には奇跡のように貴重な自然が残されており、毎日500万台近くの車輌が走り回る大都会東京の大気清浄化にわずかながら貢献しているかもしれません。**バブル経済絶頂期**の1980年代後半には皇居の地価はカリフォルニア州全体の地価に匹敵するとまでいわれました。皇居でなければとっくに開発が進み、今頃は高層ビルが林立する地帯になっていたかもしれません。

　ここは**日本のおへそ**、この国の歴史を形作った2つの大きな権力と権威を代表する徳川家と天皇家が420年余りの間、代々継承してきた千代田区千代田1丁目1番地の1です。

宮城：天皇のふだんの居所、現在は皇居と呼ぶ。

　天皇は宮城に住み神聖なる儀式を執り行い、将軍は宮城および地方の警備、軍事や紛争の調停、裁判などを担うという**二極制**が始まったのは12世紀です。その後800年近く、この体制が、緊張感をはらんだ対立、確執と和解を繰り返しながら継続したのです。そして将軍と武士

changing rooms, public baths with lockers, and sports facilities with rental running wear. The Imperial Palace Marathon, which you can enjoy immediately even if you come **empty-handed**, is truly a sacred place for runners! Miraculously much precious nature has been maintained in the verdant grounds of the Imperial Palace, which covers about 1.15 million square meters, so perhaps it also contributes, albeit in a small way, to cleansing the air in Tokyo, where almost five million vehicles ply the roads every day. In the late 1980s, at **the height of the bubble economy** in Japan, it was said that the value of the land occupied by the Imperial Palace was equivalent to that of the whole of the state of California in the United States. If the Imperial Palace were not there, most probably the area would have been redeveloped long ago and taken over by a cluster of high-rise office buildings.

The address here is 1-1-1 Chiyoda, Chiyoda-ku. It is the **navel of Japan**, a place that has been handed down from generation to generation for over 420 years by the two main forces and authorities that have shaped the history of the country, the Tokugawa family and the imperial family.

The **dual system** in which the emperor resided in the imperial palace and performed sacred ceremonies while the shogun took care of the security of the palace and the regions, military affairs, the mediation of disputes, trials, and so on began in the twelfth century. Although tense conflicts, feuds, and reconciliations occurred frequently, that system

階級の最後の舞台となったのがこの地です。日本人の得意とする**何事にも中道を行く**バランス感覚のおかげなのでしょうか、この城は将軍と天皇をそれぞれ奉る両陣営の戦場になる一歩手前で踏みとどまりました。トップ会談が開かれ、将軍が江戸城を去り、江戸城の無血開城が実現されました。将軍の城から新宮城へと姿を変えることになった1868年のことでした。

江戸城

　まずは1590年から260年余り、徳川幕府の本拠地であった江戸城の正面玄関を目指しましょう。15世紀に太田道灌が建てた江戸城は、徳川家康から3代家光までの100年間余りで日本最大の城郭に変貌しました。城の周りを「の」の字を描くように渦巻状に堀が造られ全長は26

キロ近くになりました。外堀はかなり**埋め立て**が進みましたが、内堀は今でも皇居を取り巻き、水辺には白鳥や鴨がのんびりと泳いでいます。周辺の交通渋滞でいらいらしているドライバーにひとときの安らぎを与えています。

continued for nearly 800 years. And then it was this site, where the Imperial Palace stands today, that became the final stage for the shogun and the warrior class. Perhaps thanks to that well-known Japanese sense of balance, the propensity to **always take the middle road**, Edo Castle stopped short of becoming a bloody battleground between the forces that supported the shogun and those that supported the emperor. A top-level meeting was held, the shogun left Edo Castle, and the fortress surrendered without bloodshed. The shogun's castle then became the emperor's new palace. That was in 1868.

Edo Castle

First of all, let us head to the main entrance of Edo Castle, which served as the seat of the Tokugawa shogunate for more than 260 years from 1590. Edo Castle, which was built by Ota Dokan (1432–86) in the fifteenth century, was transformed into the largest fortress in Japan over the century or so from the first Tokugawa shogun, Ieyasu (1543–1616), to the third, Iemitsu (1604–51). Moats were built in a whorl shape around the castle, eventually covering a total length of nearly 26 kilometers. The outer moats have almost completely disappeared as a result of **reclamation**, but the inner moats still surround the palace. No doubt the sight of swans and ducks swimming leisurely in the water gives drivers a moment's relief from the

さて、皇居への最寄り駅はJR東京駅です。日本に誕生した初の中央駅からスタートしましょう。

皇居と東京駅の間には丸の内とよばれる、日本を代表する大企業の本社など高層ビルが林立するビジネス街が広がっています。江戸時代にタイムスリップしてみましょう。江戸時代には、徳川家と親族関係のある親藩大名や、関ヶ原の戦いで、徳川に味方した譜代大名の屋敷が、本家江戸城**本丸**を守るように存在した地でした。その時代が終焉を迎えた後、屋敷は取り壊されたり、あるいは、大火で焼失し、このあたりは一面の藪の原野となっていたのです。この荒地を所有していた陸軍から払下げをうけ、大勝負にでたのは三菱の総裁、岩崎弥之助でした。お手本にしたのはロンドンのシティのロンバード街です。そして、21棟ものビルの設計を依頼したのはジョサイア・コンドルでした。雇われ外国人の中でもよく知られているイギリス人の筆頭です。ロンドンで生まれ、明治政府のお雇い外国人として訪日、日本の近代建築の多くの人材を育てました。日本文化にも惚れ込み、日本人の妻とともに文京区の護国寺に眠っています。

東京駅舎はコンドルの教え子である辰野金吾の設計で1914年に完成。戦災で

東京駅丸の内口

stress of traffic congestion in the vicinity.

The nearest station to the Imperial Palace is JR Tokyo Station. Let's start from the first central station ever built in Japan.

Between the Imperial Palace and Tokyo Station is a business district known as Marunouchi that is filled with skyscrapers, including the headquarters of some of Japan's largest corporations. Let's go back in time to the Edo Period. In those days, the residences of feudal lords with kinship ties to the Tokugawa family, as well as feudal lords who sided with the Tokugawa during the Battle of Sekigahara, were located in the area protecting the **main compound** of Edo Castle. After that era came to an end, the mansions were either torn down or destroyed by fire, leaving the area a thicket-covered wilderness. It was owned by the army, which sold it to Yanosuke Iwasaki, the president of Mitsubishi. The district was modeled on London's Lombard Street, and Josiah Conder was commissioned to design 21 buildings. Of all the foreigners hired by Japan, this Englishman was the most famous. Born in London, he visited Japan as a hired foreigner for the Meiji government and trained many of Japan's architectural talents of the time. He also fell in love with Japanese culture and is buried with his Japanese wife at Gokokuji Temple in Bunkyo Ward.

The Tokyo Station building was designed by Kingo Tatsuno, a student of Conder's, and was completed

焼失した３階部分などの復旧を目指した大修理が2012年に終了し、赤レンガの壁面、そこに施された白い石の横線の飾りなどが見事に蘇りました。このデザインは、辰野の独自性から「辰野式」とも言われています。往時、コンドルが丸の内に設計したいくつかの三菱のオフィスビルに準じて、イギリスのクイーン・アン様式を基礎にしたものでした。皇居側から見て長くのびた駅舎の中央にある玄関は**皇室専用**です。よく見ると、真ん中に設計者辰野がデザインした相撲の行司が持つ軍配のような模様があります。

KITTE丸の内
千代田区丸の内
2-7-2
03-3216-2811

　さて、このあたりで時間があれば立ち寄ってほしいのは、東京駅正面に向かって右側にある東京中央郵便局JPタワーに隣接する商業施設ビル、KITTE丸の内です。６階KITTEガーデンからの眺めは東京が誇れる景色です。皇居の森、行幸通り、東京駅、丸の内、八重洲地区など、明治から令和まで100年あまりの時代を経て、補修、再建、新建設されてきたさまざまな建築群が**整然と並んでいます**。新しいのに伝統がしっかり生かされている、このポイントを誇りを持って語りたいスポットです。

　それでは戻って、行幸通りを真っすぐ進めばお堀のある交差点。なおも真っす

in 1914. A major renovation project was completed in 2012 to restore the third floor and other parts of the building that were destroyed by fire in the war, and the red brick walls and the white stone horizontal lines on the walls have been beautifully restored. This design is also known as the "Tatsuno style" due to its uniqueness. It was based on the British Queen Anne style, following the style of several Mitsubishi office buildings designed by Conder in Marunouchi in the past. The entrance in the center of the station building, which stretches long from the Imperial Palace side, is **reserved for the Imperial family**. If you look closely, you can see a pattern designed by Tatsuno in the center of the building that resembles the fan of a sumo wrestling referee.

Now, if you have time in the area, stop by the KITTE Marunouchi Building, a commercial building adjacent to the Tokyo Central Post Office JP Tower on the right side facing the front of Tokyo Station. The view from the KITTE Garden on the sixth floor is one that does Tokyo proud. The Imperial Palace forest, Gyoko-dori Avenue, Tokyo Station, Marunouchi, and the Yaesu district are all **lined up in an orderly fashion**, having been repaired, rebuilt, or newly constructed over the course of more than 100 years, from the Meiji to the Showa Periods. This is a spot that I talk about with pride, as it is new but still retains a strong sense of tradition.

Then go back and go straight on Gyoko-dori to the intersection with a moat. If you walk straight, you

皇居前広場の黒松

ぐ歩くとお目当ての皇居前広場です。**形よく剪定された**黒松を見て盆栽と間違える外国人もいます。黒松といえば、大名屋敷の庭に好んで植えられた樹木のひとつです。常に変わらぬ姿の松はサムライにも好まれました。ここでタイミングよく徳川家に仕えた大名の話ができます。

19世紀中頃まではこのあたり一帯の様子は今とはまったく違っていました。会津藩松平肥後守上屋敷など大名屋敷が10棟ほど立ち並んでいました。実は今歩いてきた道、東京駅も含めて、あたり一帯は堀の内側であり、30以上の大名の上屋敷が城の本丸を守る役割も担いつつその豪華な屋敷を誇っていたところでした。現在の地名はその名残で丸の内、つまり、**城の総構**を意味する「丸」の内側ということです。

またこのあたりは掘が掘られる以前は江戸湾の入り江が広がり、東京駅も築地もまだ水の底でした。日比谷は海水が入り込む**浅瀬**で、海苔をとる杭のような「ひび」が仕込まれていたので**ひびの谷**、つまり日比谷と呼ばれました。ちなみに東京駅からひとつ目のお堀との交差点を日比谷通りに沿って左へ曲がり、3つ目の角

will find your destination, the Imperial Palace Front Gardens. Foreigners often mistake the **well-pruned** black pine trees here for *bonsai*. Speaking of black pines, the daimyo were fond of planting this tree in their residence gardens. Samurai liked them as well, because of their never-changing shape. Seizing this opportunity, now is a good time to tell foreigners about the daimyo who served the shogun.

Up to the middle of the nineteenth century this area was completely different from what it is today. It used to be occupied by about 10 residences of feudal lords, such as Matsudaira Katamori (1835–93) of the Aizu domain. In fact, the road that you have just walked along, including Tokyo Station, used to be inside the castle moats, and more than 30 daimyo had luxurious mansions here. As well as being the opulent residences of the daimyo, these mansions also had the function of protecting the main castle building, or Hon Maru. The name of the area today, Marunouchi, actually means "inside (*uchi*) the grounds and **edifice of a castle** (*maru*)."

Before the moats were dug, there was an inlet of Edo Bay in this area, and both Tokyo Station and Tsukiji were still under water. Hibiya was a **shoal** of seawater, with piles planted in order to gather laver. Hence the name Hibiya, which means "**valley** (*ya*) **of piles** (*hibi*)." Incidentally, at the first intersection with a moat from Tokyo Station, turn left along Hibiya-dori and, at the third corner on the left-hand side, you

の左側にはお城や大名屋敷を火事から守る消防隊の屋敷がありました。上級消防士、火消し同心の子供としてこの地で生まれたのが浮世絵絵師、歌川広重です。**生粋の江戸っ子**です。名所江戸百景や東海道五十三次などの浮世絵で知られる海外でも人気の高い絵師、広重の誕生の地です。

　皇居前広場を横切る内堀通りに出ます。桔梗門（ききょうもん）や坂下門は数ある江戸城への入り口でした。内堀の角に建つのが**巽櫓**（たつみやぐら）です。東京で唯一真近に見られる日本の城郭建築のひとつであり、特徴ある漆喰（しっくい）総塗り壁、石落とし用出窓、鉄砲や弓を撃つ狭間が見られます。遠方に見える富士見櫓にもご注目。1659年に建てられた3層の櫓です。1657年の大火で消失した天守閣に変わって江戸城のシンボル的櫓として現存し、今に至っています。

東御苑

　正門である大手門へはお堀に沿って北へ進みます。少し左へカーブすればすぐです。大名たちが登城する際は必ずこの門で下乗して入城しました。皇宮警察官

come to the site of a former fire brigade residence that protected Edo Castle and the daimyo mansions from fire. This was the birthplace of Utagawa Hiroshige (1797–1858), the famous ukiyo-e painter whose father was a fireman. In other words, Hiroshige was a **genuine Edokko** (child of Edo). Hiroshige is a popular artist both in Japan and overseas for such works as the *Meisho Edo Hyakkei* (One Hundred Views of Edo) and *Tokaido Gojusantsugi* (Fifty-Three Stations of the Tokaido Road).

Go out onto Uchibori-dori, which cuts across the Imperial Palace Plaza. Kikyomon Gate was one of the many entrances to Edo Castle. There is a **watchtower**, Tatsumiyagura, standing at the corner of the moat. This is one of the few places in Tokyo where you can actually see Japanese castle architecture close at hand. There is the characteristic plastered wall, bay windows for dropping stones, and loopholes for guns and bows. You can see Fujimi Tower in the distance, too. This three-storied watchtower, which was built in 1659, became the symbol of Edo Castle in place of the castle tower, which was burned down in the great fire of 1657, and it still serves in that role today.

Eastern Garden

Head north, following the moat, toward Otemon, which is the main gate. If you turn to the left slightly, you will soon come to it. It was here that, when visiting the castle, the daimyo would alight from their

のにこやかな挨拶を受けながら大名気分で本丸への道筋をたどります。お目当ては東御苑の二の丸庭園です。

大手門は城の表玄関です。敵の集中攻撃を受ける可能性が高い場所なので、敵のさらなる進行を防ぐため、門内は枡形（ますがた）と呼ばれる防御施設になっています。高麗門（らいもん）と呼ばれる一番目の門を入ってきた敵は、四方を囲まれ、身動きができなくなります。そこへ上から、横からと火を放つなどの攻撃をしかけるのです。高麗門の一部は由緒ある江戸時代からの**遺構**（こう）で、銅板により防火補強されています。正門にふさわしい頑強なつくりとなっています。

門を通り過ぎて左へ曲がったところに警備受付があるので、そこでプラスチックの入城札を受け取ってください。真っすぐ進んで次の城門跡の石垣の間を進むと長い百人番所があり、ここで大きく右へ曲がると目の前に高い石垣です。主に安山岩でできており、上に向かって曲線を描く美しさに当時の土木技術の高さが実感されます。

右側の雑木林を通路に沿って抜けたところに、高名な庭師の小堀遠州作といわれている二の丸庭園が復元されました。

百人番所：大手門から本丸に入るときに最大の検問所。警備をまかされた各組には同心が百人ずつ配属されたという。

palanquins and enter. The smiling faces of the guards as they greet you will no doubt make you feel like a lord yourself as you enter. Our target here is the Ninomaru Garden in the Eastern Garden.

Since the Otemon Gate was the main entrance to the castle, it was highly likely to come under intensive attack from the enemy. In order to prevent the enemy's forward advance, therefore, it was structured in the shape of a *masu*, a cubic receptacle used for measuring liquids. Such gates are therefore described as *masugata*. If the enemy entered the first gate, which was called the "Korean Gate," they would find themselves trapped in a space shut off on all sides. Defenders of the castle could then fire on them from above and from the sides. Part of the "Korean Gate" is a **remnant** from the Edo Period and has been reinforced with sheet copper to prevent fire. It is a very stout structure, befitting the main entrance to the castle.

Pass through the gate, turn left, and take a plastic token from the security reception. Then proceed straight ahead and, passing between the stone walls of other gateway sites, you will reach the long Hundred-Person Guardhouse. Turn sharply to the right here, and there will be a high stone wall in front of you. This wall is made mainly of andesite. The beautiful curves stretching upward are impressive and attest to the high level of engineering at that time.

Following the path through the grove of trees on the right, you will come to a reproduction of the Ninomaru Garden, which is said to have been

春はしだれ桜、続いて紫陽花、菖蒲、藤、夏は百日紅、秋は紅葉、冬は椿と四季おりおりの花で出迎えてくれる将軍の庭です。時間があれば、先ほどの石垣に戻って汐見坂を登り本丸跡を訪れてみてください。天守閣跡に登り、**天下取り気分を味わってひと休みです。**

汐見坂：本丸と二の丸をつなぐ坂道で、昔はこの辺りまで日比谷の入り江が入り込んでいたため、坂から海を眺めることができた。

二重橋

　大手門に戻ってお堀端を東京タワー方面へ向かって歩き、もう一度、巽櫓、その先の桔梗門、坂下門を見ながら10分ほどで二重橋に到着です。手前の石橋と後方の鉄橋が総称で二重橋と呼ばれています。徳川家が城を去った後、江戸城は東京城となり、16歳の明治天皇が京都から移り住むことになります。新宮城は江戸城の本丸跡地ではなく、西の丸跡地に建てられました。西の丸への門が宮城への正門となり、二重橋となって今に至っています。眼鏡橋とも呼ばれる石橋をバックに**記念写真**をお忘れなく。

originally designed for the shogun by the famous landscape gardener Kobori Enshu (1579–1647). The shogun's garden offers colorful blossoms throughout the year: weeping cherry trees in spring, followed by hydrangea, irises, and wisteria; crape myrtles in summer; maples in autumn; and camellia in winter. If you have time, go back to the stone wall and climb up Shiomizaka ("tide-viewing slope") to see the site of the Hon Maru, the castle's main fortress. Having made the ascent, treat yourself to a rest and **savor what it feels like to be king** for a moment.

Nijubashi

Go back to the Otemon Gate and follow the moat in the direction of Tokyo Tower. You will pass the watchtower and Kikyomon and Sakashitamon gates again and then, in about ten minutes, reach Nijubashi ("double-layer bridge"). This is the name given to two bridges, a stone bridge at the front and an iron bridge behind. After the Tokugawa family had left the castle, Edo Castle became Tokyo Castle, and the 16-year-old Emperor Meiji moved here from Kyoto. A new palace for him was built not on the site of the Hon Maru but on the site of the Nishi no Maru. The gate to the Nishi no Maru, and the Nijubashi Bridge, became the main entrance to the new palace. Don't forget to take a **commemorative photo** with the stone bridge, which is called "eyeglass bridge," in the background.

日本の天皇の地位は7世紀頃には確立していたといわれます。隋書倭国伝によると、当時の皇子であった聖徳太子が送った遣隋使の国書に、「日出づる処の天子、書を日没する処の天子にいたす」、また日本書記には「東の天皇、敬しみて西の皇帝にもうす」という文言があったとのことです。天皇という名称が初めて使われ、内外にその存在を表明したわけです。現代のデリケートな日中関係を思うと、古代の人々の**堂々とした威厳に満ちた発言**に驚きます。

The position of the emperor of Japan is said to have been established in about the seventh century. According to a Chinese historical document, the *Kenzuishi no Kokusho* (Diplomatic Message of the Embassies to the Sui Dynasty, which was sent by Prince Shotoku [574–622]), stated, "The Emperor in the land where the sun rises addresses the Emperor in the land where the sun sets." And in the *Nihon Shoki* (Chronicle of Japan) it is written that "The Emperor of the east respectfully speaks to the Emperor of the west." In consideration of the delicate state of relations between Japan and China at present, the **extremely bold and majestic statements** that people made in ancient times seem quite surprising.

その後、万世一系の天皇家の血筋は現在の126代令和天皇まで**存続**し、現日本国憲法で国民の象徴としてその存在が認められています。国民の多くが天皇家の存在には好意的な気持ちを持っているようです。世界にもあまり**例を見ない**長い歴史を生きてきた天皇家です。年に2度、この二重橋を渡って一般庶民が新宮殿に参賀できる機会があります。事前申請で予約する、あるいは決められた時間（午前9時〜9時半、午後12時半〜1時）に当日受付で予約なしでの皇居見学もできます。その際は外国人はパスポートが必要なのでお忘れなく。そして、本人確認も不要なのは4月の乾通りの一般公開です。4月といえば、もちろん桜見物です。皇居のそれはあくまでも上品に桜を愛でます。飲めや歌えのお花見ではないので、くれぐれもご注意を！

　二重橋を背にして真っすぐ進み、右に曲がると芝生の一角に大きな銅像があります。アメリカ映画のスターウォーズに出てくるダース・ベイダーに似た兜をかぶった馬上のサムライは楠正成です。14世紀、武家の政治に異を唱え、天皇による政治の復権を願って画策し、失敗し、無念の死をとげた後醍醐天皇。その天皇の**忠臣**として知られる武将です。馬を駆

Since then, the Japanese imperial line has been **continued unbroken** (the current emperor, Emperor Naruhito, is the 126th sovereign in the traditional count), and the imperial family has a long history probably **unparalleled** by other monarchies in the world. Generally speaking, most Japanese people seem to have favorable feelings toward the imperial family, and twice a year ordinary citizens have the opportunity to cross the Nijubashi Bridge and offer congratulations to the imperial family at the Kyuden. You can make a reservation by applying in advance, or you can visit the Imperial Palace without a reservation on the day of your visit at the designated times (9:00 to 9:30 a.m. and 12:30 to 1:00 p.m.). Do not forget that foreigners need their passports for this. Additionally, ID checks are not required when Inui-dori Street, the road through the palace grounds, is opened to the public in April. In April, of course, you can see the cherry blossoms, but at the Imperial Palace, you can enjoy them in an elegant way. It is not a cherry blossom viewing party where you can drink and sing, so be careful!

Leaving Nijubashi behind you, go straight ahead and then turn right. You will see a big bronze statue standing in a corner. The samurai on horseback, who is wearing a helmet like that of Darth Vader in the US movie series *Star Wars*, is Kusunoki Masashige (1294–1336). Masashige was a **loyal follower** of Emperor Go Daigo (1288–1339), who objected to rule by the shogunate, plotted to restore imperial rule, failed, and met a somewhat disheartening death. The statue of

けて天皇を救うべく走っている姿が銅像になりました。日本が近代化へとまっしぐらに走り始めた明治時代、当時日本を代表する彫刻家だった高村光雲の1900年の作です。

　ところで日本の天皇がなぜ1300年あまり天皇であり続けられたのか？　この大きな疑問にはどのように答えたらよいのでしょうか。ここで再登場するのは日本独特のバランス感覚です。12世紀から武士階級が政治、経済、軍事を担い始めたとき、天皇は国の伝統文化的行事や自然と人間との深いかかわりを宗教化したともいえる日本古来の神道の儀礼を執り行い、継承する役割を担うことで**権威の保持に努めた**のです。権力を求めて武士が戦い続けている間、天皇家は京都の宮城にとどまり続けました。武士が歴史から消えていった後も、天皇家が存続できた理由のひとつではないでしょうか。

　さて、東京のガイドはここ皇居にてひとまずお別れです。常に進化しつづける東京は、その**見所**も変化しています。観るだけでなく、体験したり、名物料理を楽しんだり、楽しみ方は千差万別です。東京を思いきり満喫する旅を楽しんでいただけることを心から願って、Have a nice day!

Masashige galloping to help the emperor, finished in 1900, is the work of Koun Takamura (1852–1934), a leading sculptor in the Meiji Era, when Japan was beginning its furious dash toward modernization.

People often ask why the Japanese imperial system has continued for 1,300 years or so. The answer probably lies, once again, in the unique sense of balance of the Japanese. When the warrior class began to control political, economic, and military affairs from the twelfth century, the emperor **endeavored to maintain his authority** by taking on a role of performing and passing down traditional cultural events of the state and ceremonies of Shinto, Japan's indigenous ancient religion that focuses on the deep relationship between nature and humankind. While the warlords continued to fight one another in their pursuit of power, the imperial family remained in the Imperial Palace in Kyoto. This might be one of the reasons why the imperial family was able to survive even after the samurai disappeared from history.

Now, our guide to Tokyo will leave us here at the Imperial Palace. Tokyo is constantly evolving, and its **attractions** are changing as well. There are so many different ways to enjoy Tokyo, not only by seeing it, but also by experiencing it and enjoying its food specialties. I sincerely hope that you will enjoy your trip to fully enjoy Tokyo, and have a nice day!

English Conversational Ability Test
国際英語会話能力検定

● E-CATとは…
英語が話せるようになるための
テストです。インターネット
ベースで、30分であなたの発
話力をチェックします。

www.ecatexam.com

● iTEP®とは…
世界各国の企業、政府機関、アメリカの大学
300校以上が、英語能力判定テストとして採用。
オンラインによる90分のテストで文法、リー
ディング、リスニング、ライティング、スピー
キングの5技能をスコア化。iTEP®は、留学、就
職、海外赴任などに必要な、世界に通用する英
語力を総合的に評価する画期的なテストです。

www.itepexamjapan.com

［対訳ニッポン双書］

通訳ガイドがナビする東京歩き【新版】
Tokyo: A Walking Tour

2009年7月11日　第1版第1刷発行
2014年5月6日　第2版第1刷発行
2021年5月8日　第3版第1刷発行

著　者　松岡　明子

訳　者　ジョン・タラント

発行者　浦　　晋亮

発行所　**IBCパブリッシング株式会社**
〒162-0804 東京都新宿区中里町29番3号 菱秀神楽坂ビル9F
Tel. 03-3513-4511　Fax. 03-3513-4512
www.ibcpub.co.jp

印刷所　**株式会社シナノパブリッシングプレス**

© 松岡明子 2009, 2014, 2021
© IBC Publishing, Inc. 2009, 2014, 2021

Printed in Japan

落丁本・乱丁本は、小社宛にお送りください。送料小社負担にてお取り替えいたします。
本書の無断複写（コピー）は著作権法上での例外を除き禁じられています。

ISBN978-4-7946-0658-7

企画・編集協力＝社団法人 国際交流サービス協会
政府等が海外から招聘する外国人の受入業務や、駐日各国大使館員に対する日本文化紹介事業等を行っている
外務省所管の公益法人。1970年設立
撮影＝君和田富美夫